BAGS™

(OR A STORY THEREOF)

Published by
ARCHAIA™

BAGS (OR A STORY THEREOF), July 2019. Published by Archaia, a division of Boom Entertainment, Inc. Bags (or a story thereof) is ™ and © Patrick McHale. All rights reserved. Archaia™ and the Archaia logo are trademarks of Boom Entertainment, Inc., registered in various countries and categories. All characters, events, and institutions depicted herein are fictional. Any similarity between any of the names, characters, persons, and/or institutions in this publication to actual names, characters, and persons, whether living or dead, events, and/or institutions is unintended and purely coincidental.

BOOM! Studios, 5670 Wilshire Boulevard, Suite 400, Los Angeles, CA 90036-5679. Printed in Canada. First Printing.

ISBN: 978-1-68415-409-8, eISBN: 978-1-64144-462-0

BAGS

™

(OR A STORY THEREOF)

CREATED BY **PATRICK McHALE**

ADAPTED & ILLUSTRATED BY **GAVIN FULLERTON**

COLORS BY **WHITNEY COGAR**

LETTERS BY **MARIE ENGER**

COVER BY **GAVIN FULLERTON**
WITH COLORS BY **WHITNEY COGAR**

DESIGNER **JILLIAN CRAB**

ASSISTANT EDITOR **MICHAEL MOCCIO**

EDITOR **SHANNON WATTERS**
WITH SPECIAL THANKS TO **WHITNEY LEOPARD**

FOREWORD

Hello, my name is Patrick McHale. I wrote the original story that this comic is based on, and I was asked to write a little bit about how the story came to be.

For most of my career I have worked in TV animation—I'm mostly known for creating the miniseries *Over the Garden Wall*—but, at a certain point, I ran away from Los Angeles to live in upstate New York. At the time, I wasn't sure if I'd ever work in animation again, and I needed to figure out another career option for myself. My wife suggested I be a novelist. I thought that seemed like a good thing to be. Then I could say, "Oh, have you read my novel?"

I didn't know much about novelists, but I presumed that most of them tended to write a lot of words really quickly. So, if I wanted to be a real novelist, and actually make a living at it, I knew I would need to be very prolific. I decided to write my first novel in one week to prove to myself I could really do it.

Not knowing how to start writing a novel, and not particularly enjoying the beginning of most novels myself, I started *Bags* as simply as I could: "Once there was a man who was looking for his dog." What a terrible opening line for a novel! But it cut right to the chase, and it got me off and running with a simple premise that could lead just about anywhere.

By the end of the week, I was finished writing my story. But it wasn't exactly the *New York Times* bestselling thriller that I had imagined when I'd started. It was a weird and awkwardly written story involving a talking walrus, a full grown man who's afraid of children, and a very lonesome Devil living in a house made of bones. Worst of all, it was only about 4,600 words long! A real novel is at least 50,000 words! I had failed! Miserably! Yet, for some reason, I still kind of liked the thing.

I spent about a month editing the book, elaborating certain parts and doing artwork to pad it out. It was some of the most fun I've ever had working on a project, because there was no audience. I could just experiment. By the end of the month, the book was 54 pages in length, with HUGE margins and a bunch of illustrations. I was certainly no novelist, but for some reason I was proud of the little book I'd made. It was my first book, and it was the longest story I'd ever written at that point. So, although the style of writing was odd and experimental— my friend Max referred to it as "a satire of bad writing", which was only partially intentional, haha—and the illustrations were essentially drawn with my eyes closed, and the story was very, very short...the whole thing was still rather special to me.

I also had the idea to call up my friend Andrew Dorsett and have him write a soundtrack for the book, something people could listen to while reading. Those plans came to a halt when I suddenly got the opportunity to make a pilot for Cartoon Network, which eventually turned into my miniseries *Over the Garden Wall*. As I began to write that series, and structure the overarching story, I found that the experience of writing *Bags* helped me substantially. There's even a narrative flashback device in *Over the Garden Wall* that I stole directly from *Bags*.

After *Over the Garden Wall* ended, I finally had the time to officially release *Bags*. Andrew, along with our friend Eli Moore, put the soundtrack together, I got the books printed, and we started selling them online. The soundtrack is still available! You can find it here:

somebooks.bandcamp.com

Eventually, comic book editor Whitney Leopard reached out to me about having the story adapted into a graphic novel. I wasn't sure at first; the book was weird, and it wasn't written for any particular audience in mind. I wasn't sure how it would be received by wider audiences, or if it would work in a comic book format. But in the same spirit of experimentation that was always part of this story, we decided to do it! And I'm glad we did. Gavin Fullerton took on the challenge of adapting and illustrating the story, and he—along with colorist Whitney Cogar and letterer Marie Enger—really brought *Bags* to life in new ways, while also capturing all the best stuff from my weird little book.

I hope you enjoy this comic, and that the rest of your life is good, too.

Yours truly,

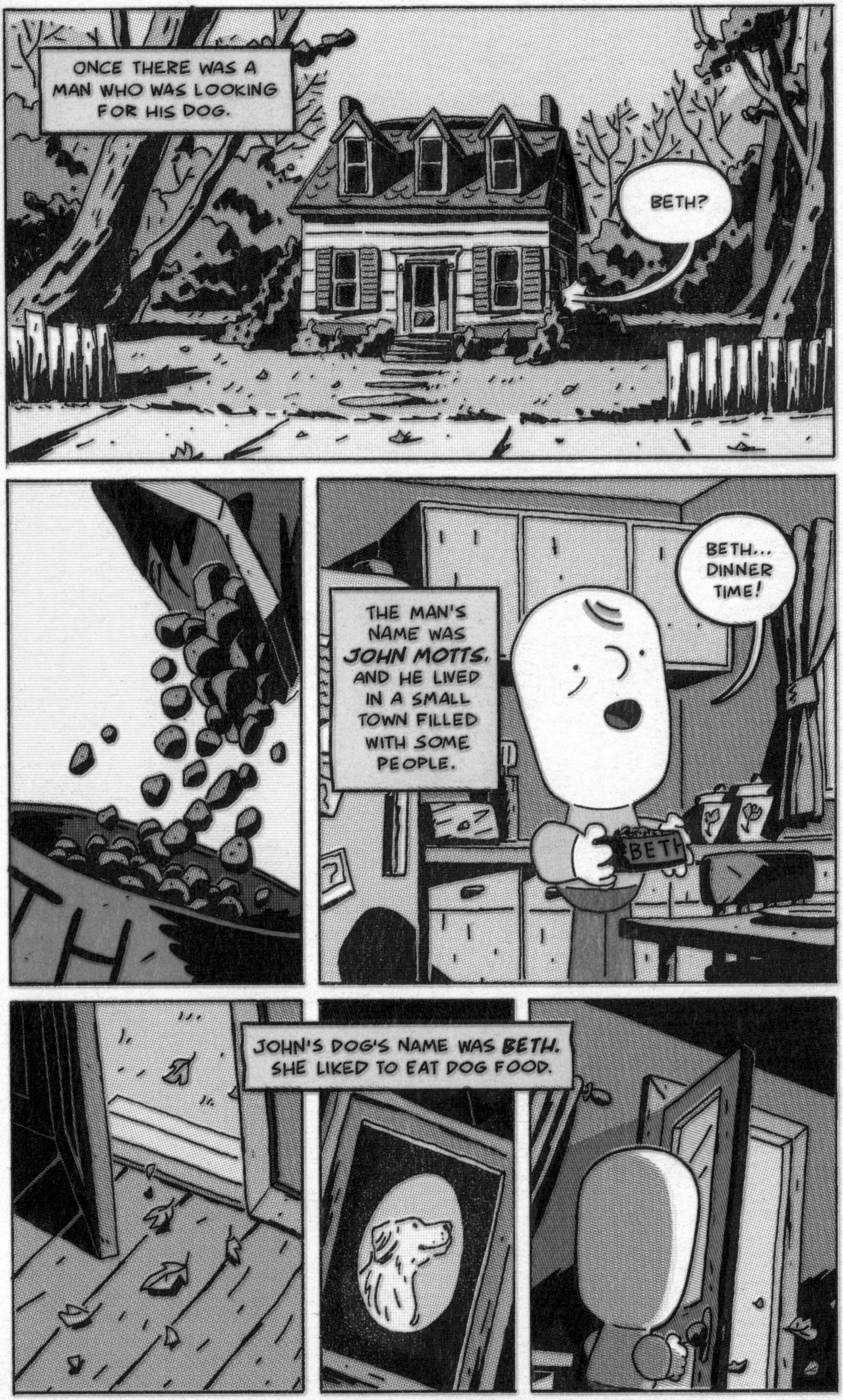
ONCE THERE WAS A MAN WHO WAS LOOKING FOR HIS DOG.
BETH?
THE MAN'S NAME WAS JOHN MOTTS, AND HE LIVED IN A SMALL TOWN FILLED WITH SOME PEOPLE.
BETH... DINNER TIME!
BETH
JOHN'S DOG'S NAME WAS BETH. SHE LIKED TO EAT DOG FOOD.

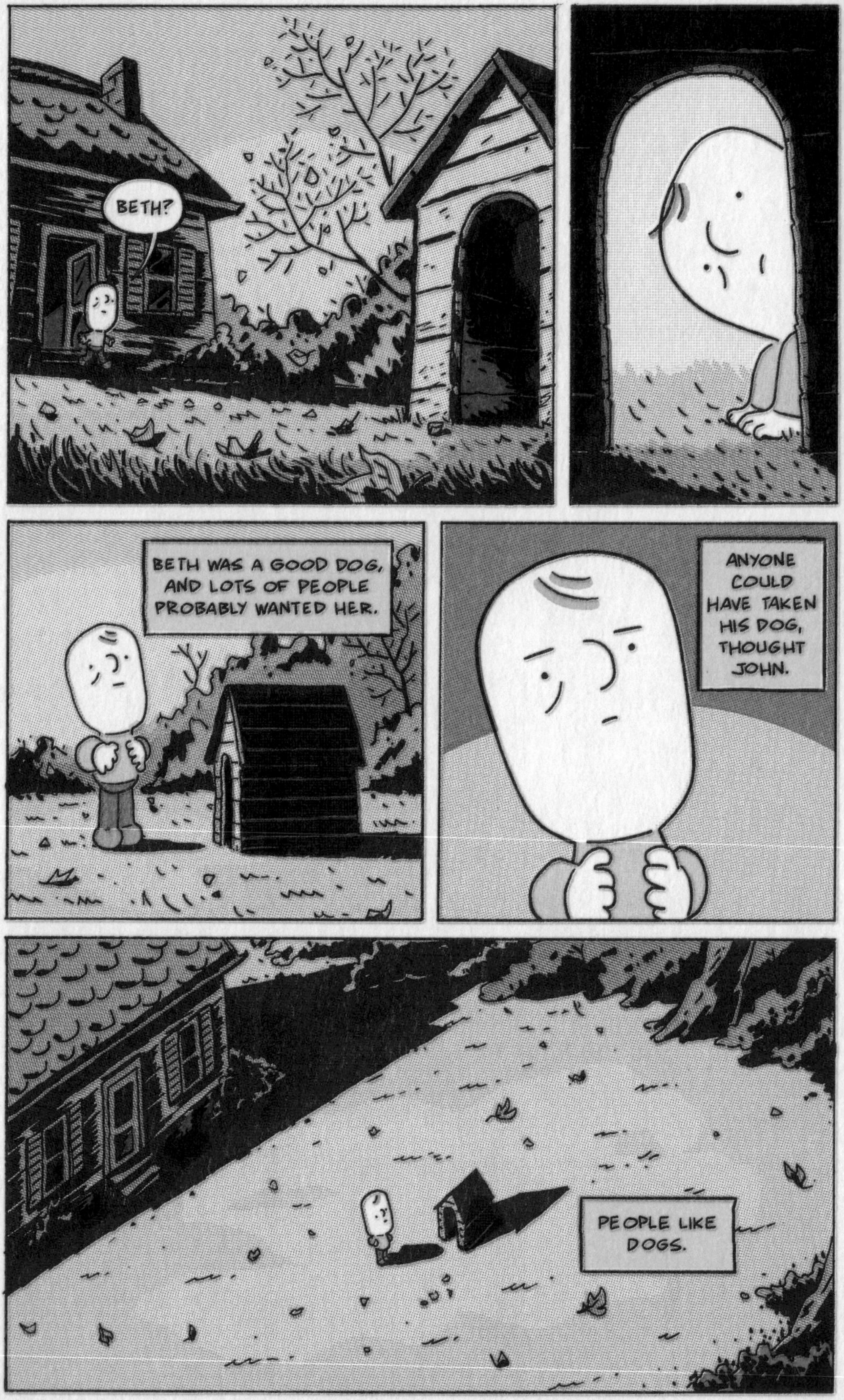
BETH?
BETH WAS A GOOD DOG, AND LOTS OF PEOPLE PROBABLY WANTED HER.
ANYONE COULD HAVE TAKEN HIS DOG, THOUGHT JOHN.
PEOPLE LIKE DOGS.

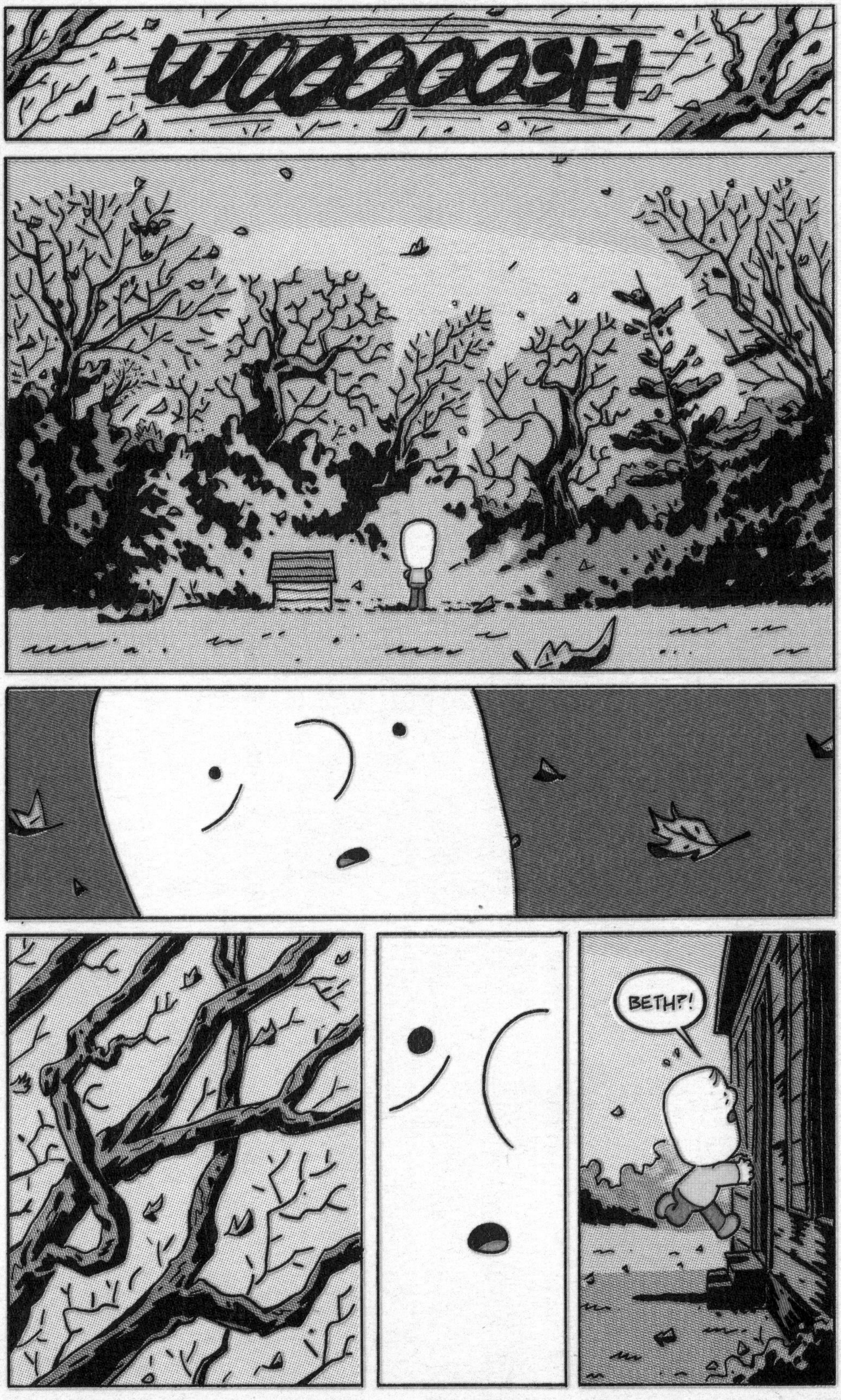
WOOOOOOSH
BETH?!

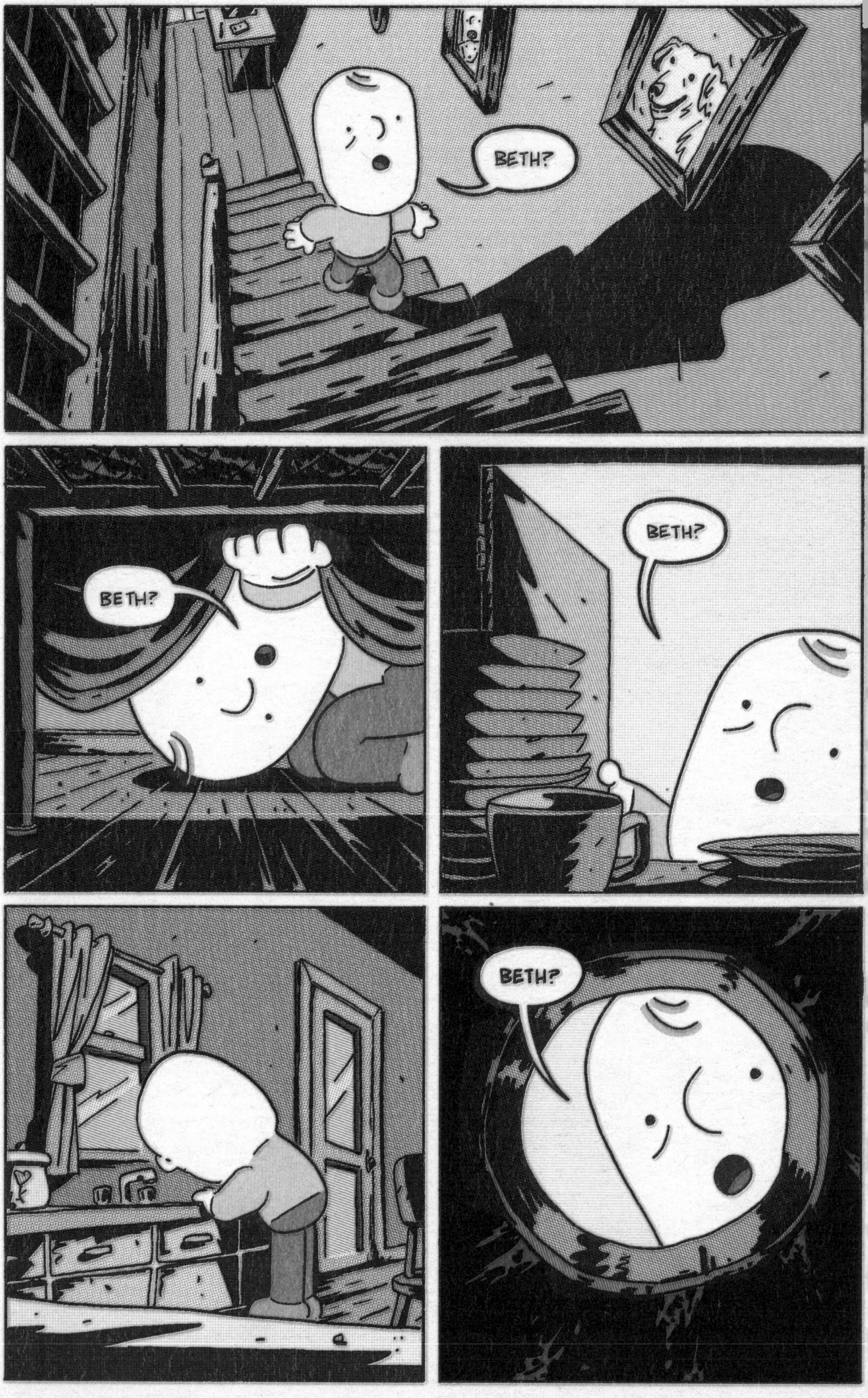
BETH?
BETH?
BETH?
BETH?

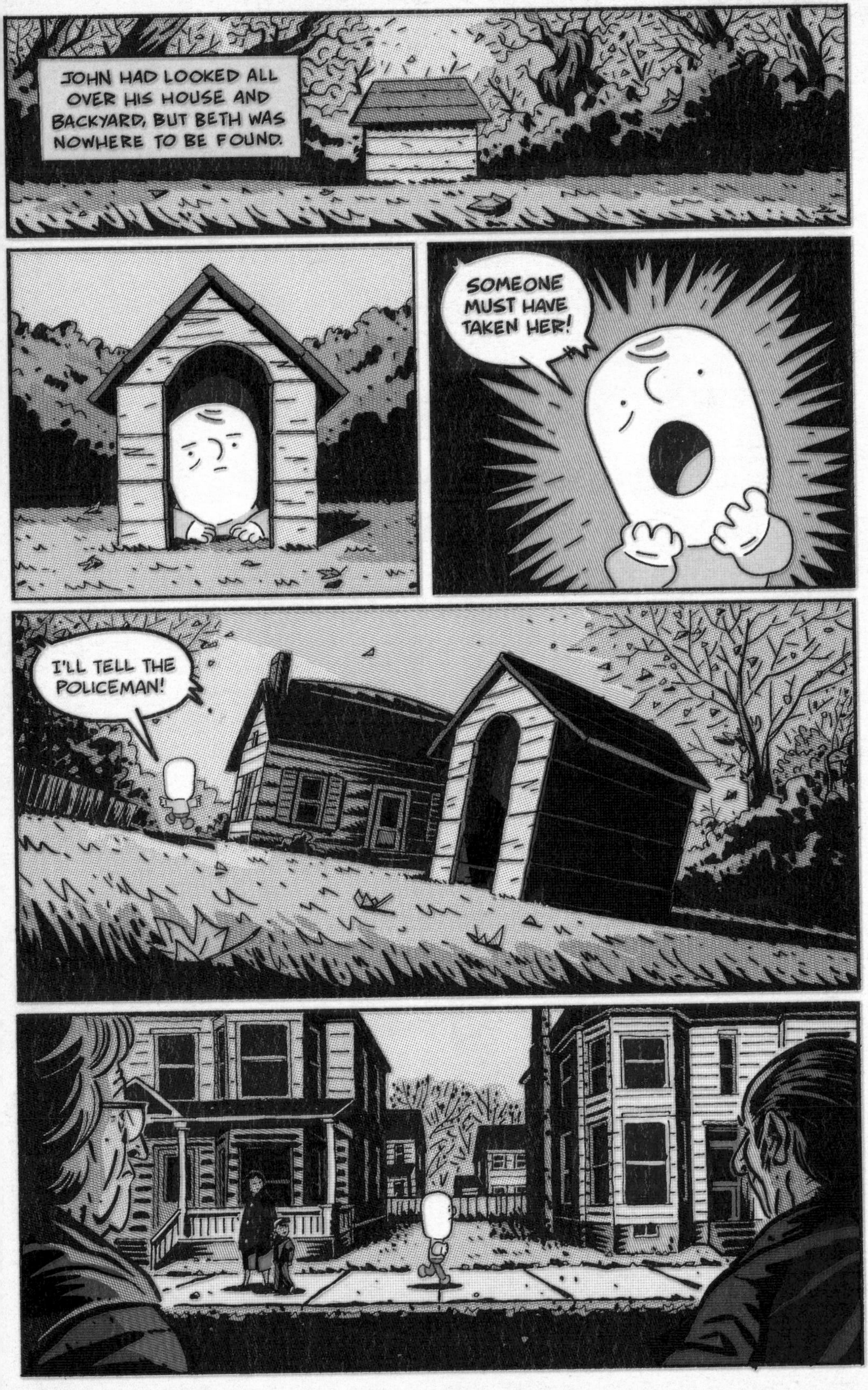
JOHN HAD LOOKED ALL OVER HIS HOUSE AND BACKYARD, BUT BETH WAS NOWHERE TO BE FOUND.
SOMEONE MUST HAVE TAKEN HER!
I'LL TELL THE POLICEMAN!

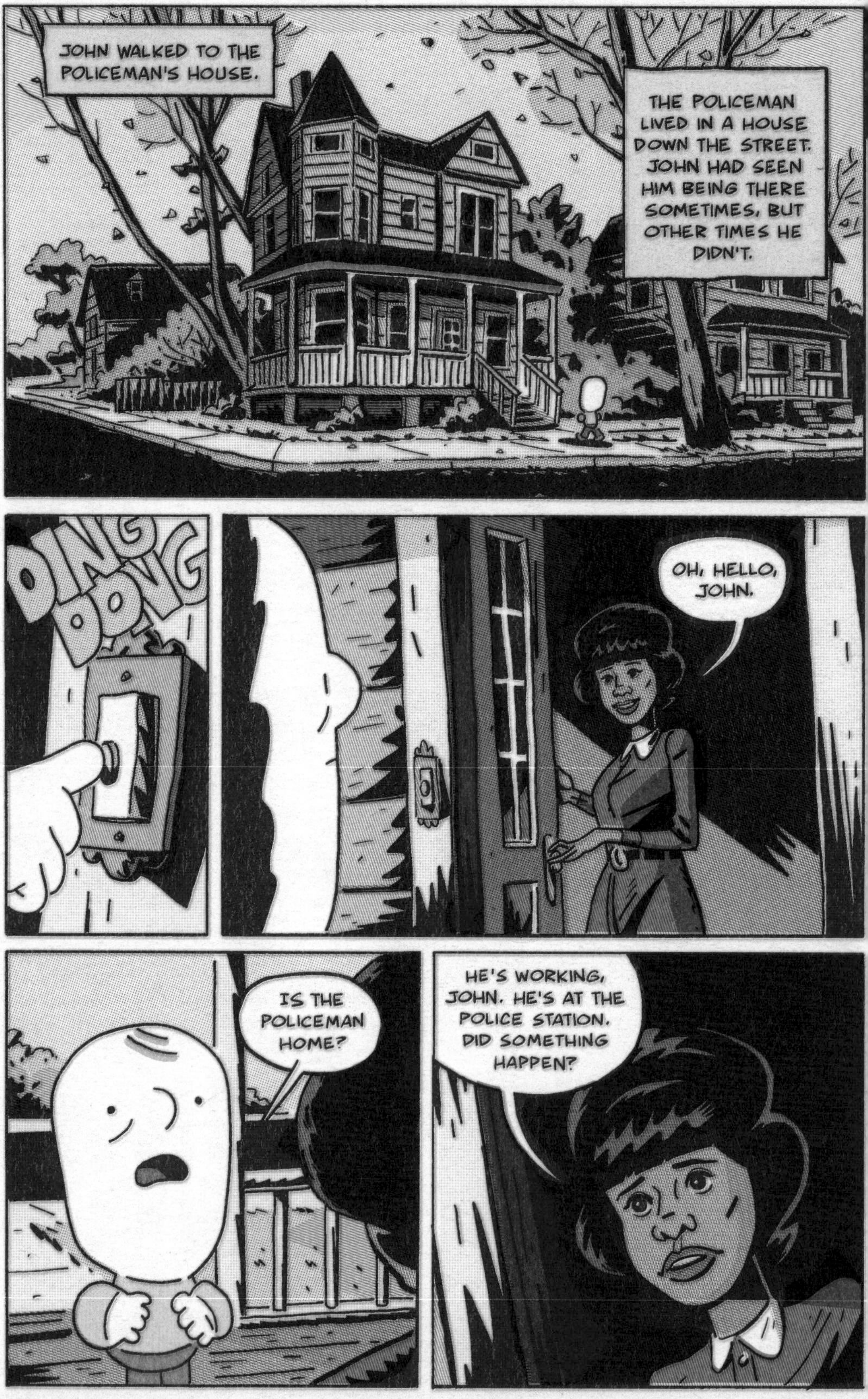
JOHN WALKED TO THE POLICEMAN'S HOUSE.
THE POLICEMAN LIVED IN A HOUSE DOWN THE STREET. JOHN HAD SEEN HIM BEING THERE SOMETIMES, BUT OTHER TIMES HE DIDN'T.
DING DONG
OH, HELLO, JOHN.
IS THE POLICEMAN HOME?
HE'S WORKING, JOHN. HE'S AT THE POLICE STATION. DID SOMETHING HAPPEN?

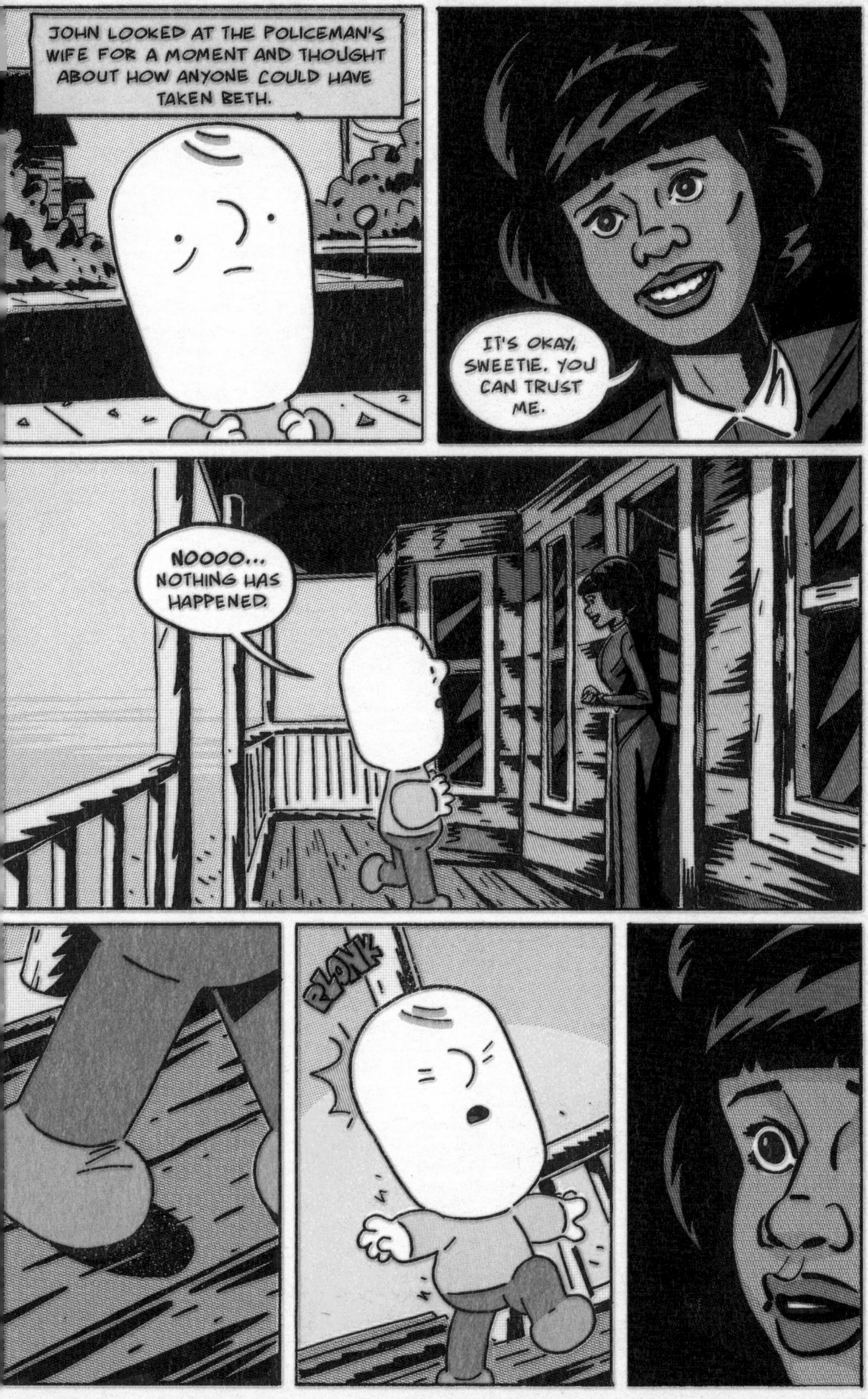
JOHN LOOKED AT THE POLICEMAN'S WIFE FOR A MOMENT AND THOUGHT ABOUT HOW ANYONE COULD HAVE TAKEN BETH.
IT'S OKAY, SWEETIE. YOU CAN TRUST ME.
NOOOO... NOTHING HAS HAPPENED.
PLONK

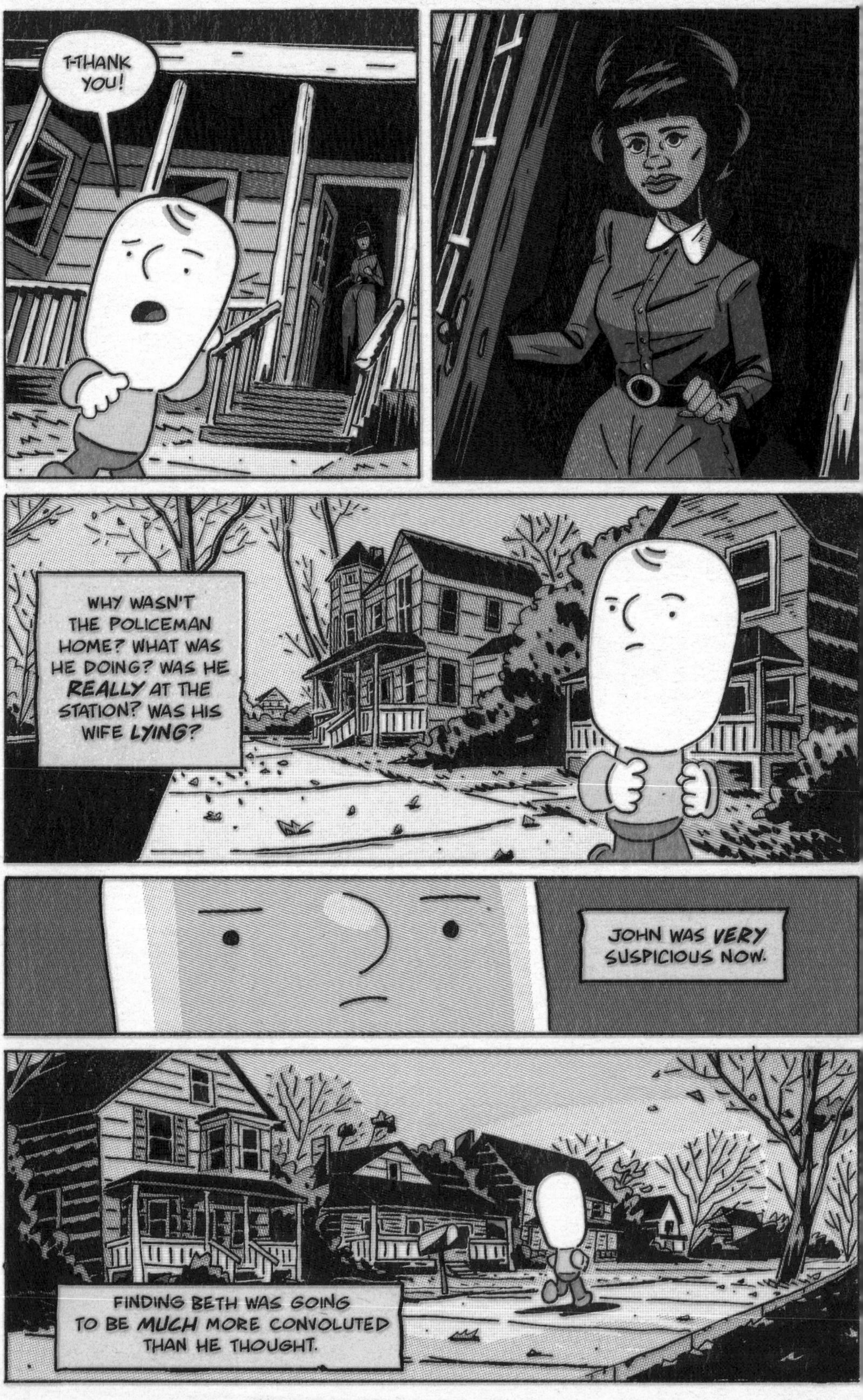

T-THANK YOU!
WHY WASN'T THE POLICEMAN HOME? WHAT WAS HE DOING? WAS HE REALLY AT THE STATION? WAS HIS WIFE LYING?
JOHN WAS VERY SUSPICIOUS NOW.
FINDING BETH WAS GOING TO BE MUCH MORE CONVOLUTED THAN HE THOUGHT.

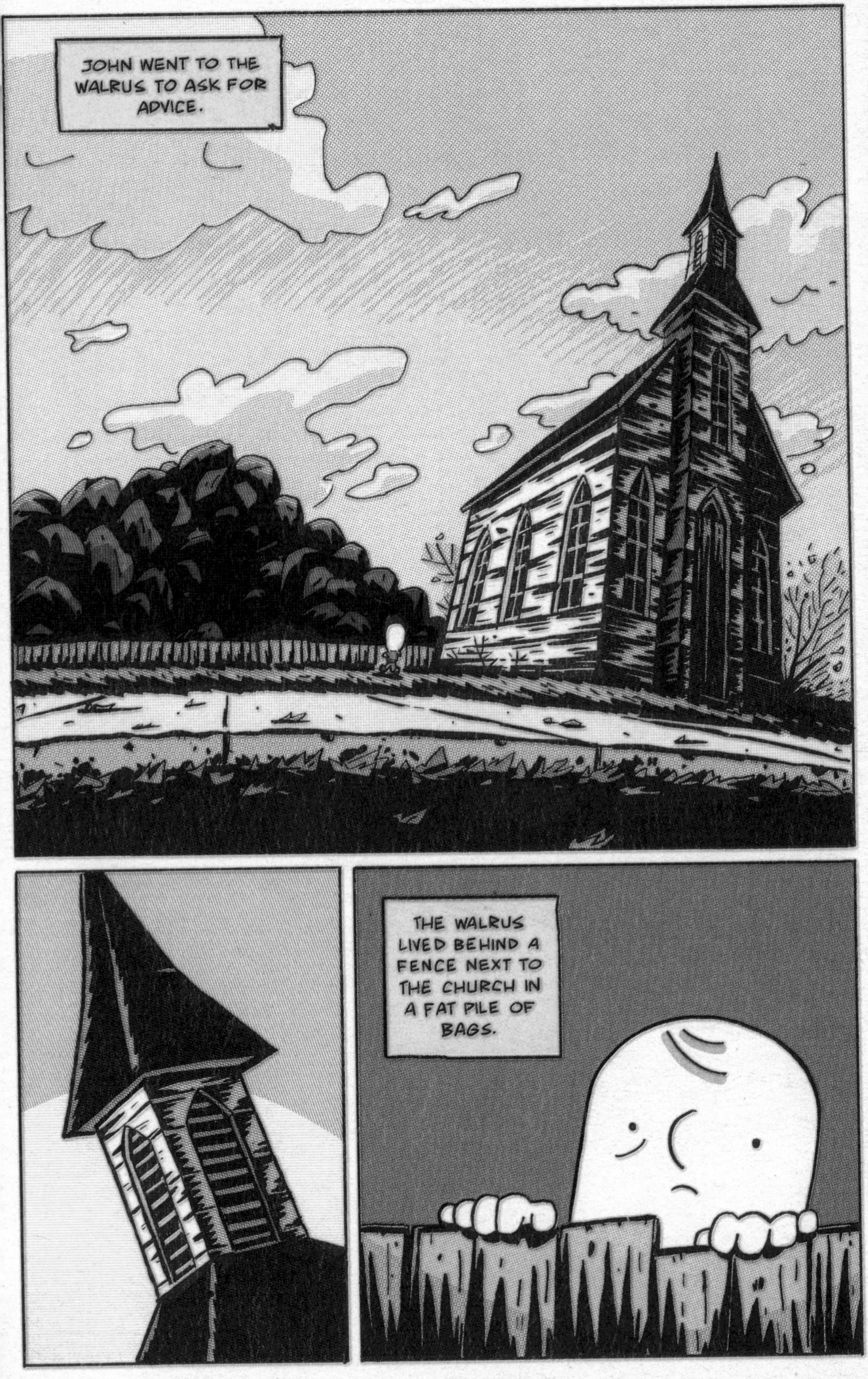
JOHN WENT TO THE WALRUS TO ASK FOR ADVICE.
THE WALRUS LIVED BEHIND A FENCE NEXT TO THE CHURCH IN A FAT PILE OF BAGS.

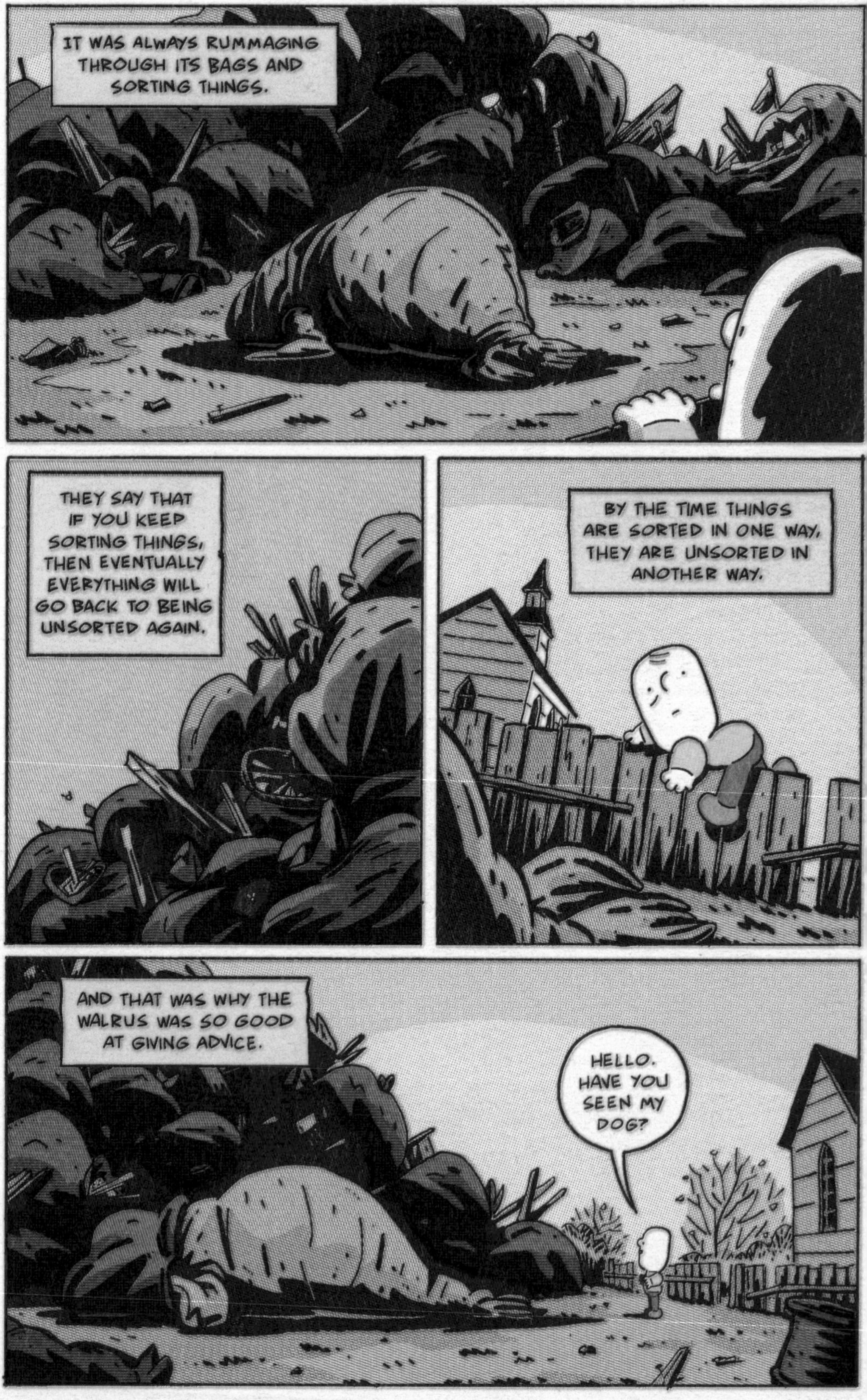
IT WAS ALWAYS RUMMAGING THROUGH ITS BAGS AND SORTING THINGS.
THEY SAY THAT IF YOU KEEP SORTING THINGS, THEN EVENTUALLY EVERYTHING WILL GO BACK TO BEING UNSORTED AGAIN.
BY THE TIME THINGS ARE SORTED IN ONE WAY, THEY ARE UNSORTED IN ANOTHER WAY.
AND THAT WAS WHY THE WALRUS WAS SO GOOD AT GIVING ADVICE.
HELLO. HAVE YOU SEEN MY DOG?

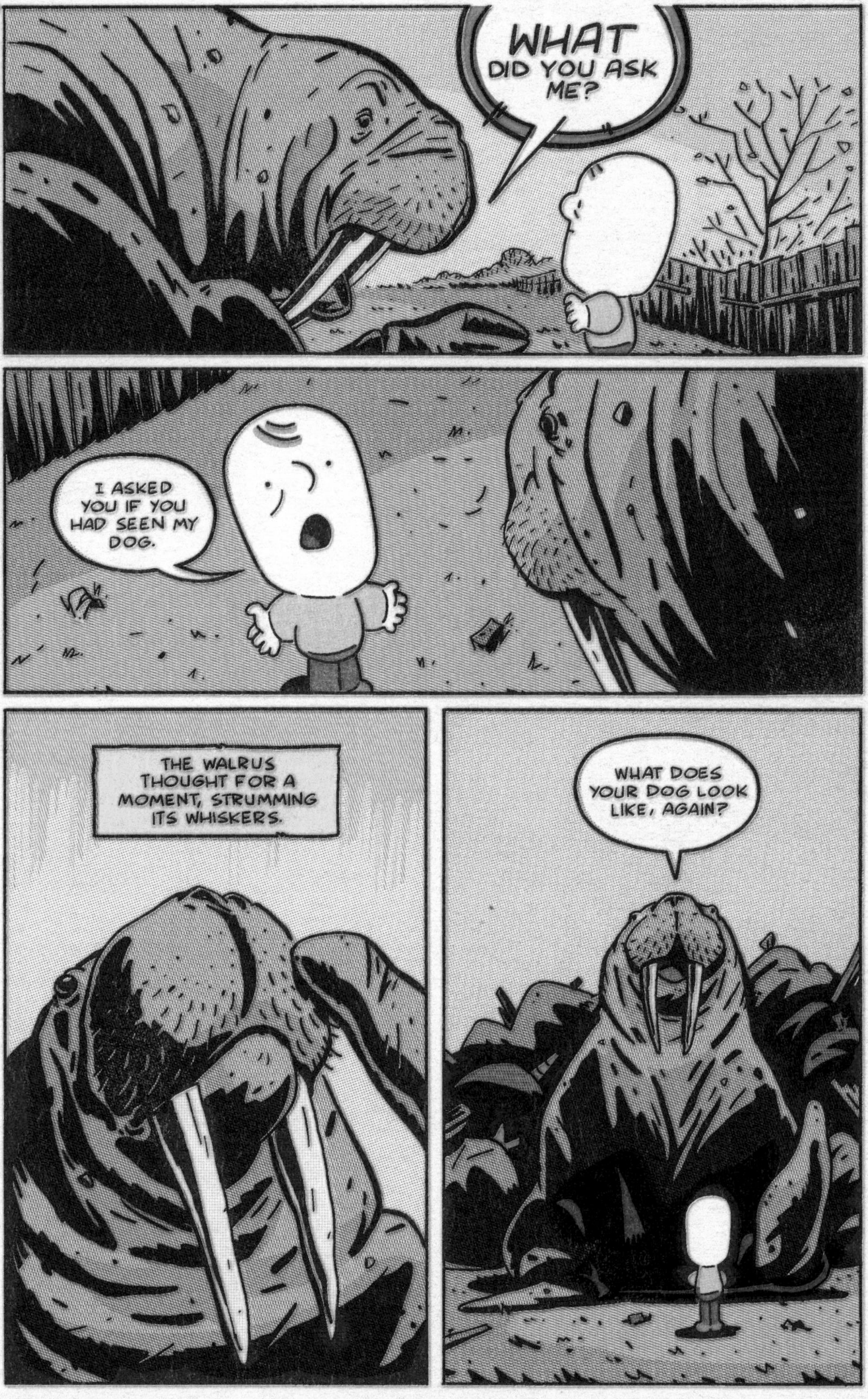
WHAT DID YOU ASK ME?
I ASKED YOU IF YOU HAD SEEN MY DOG.
THE WALRUS THOUGHT FOR A MOMENT, STRUMMING ITS WHISKERS.
WHAT DOES YOUR DOG LOOK LIKE, AGAIN?

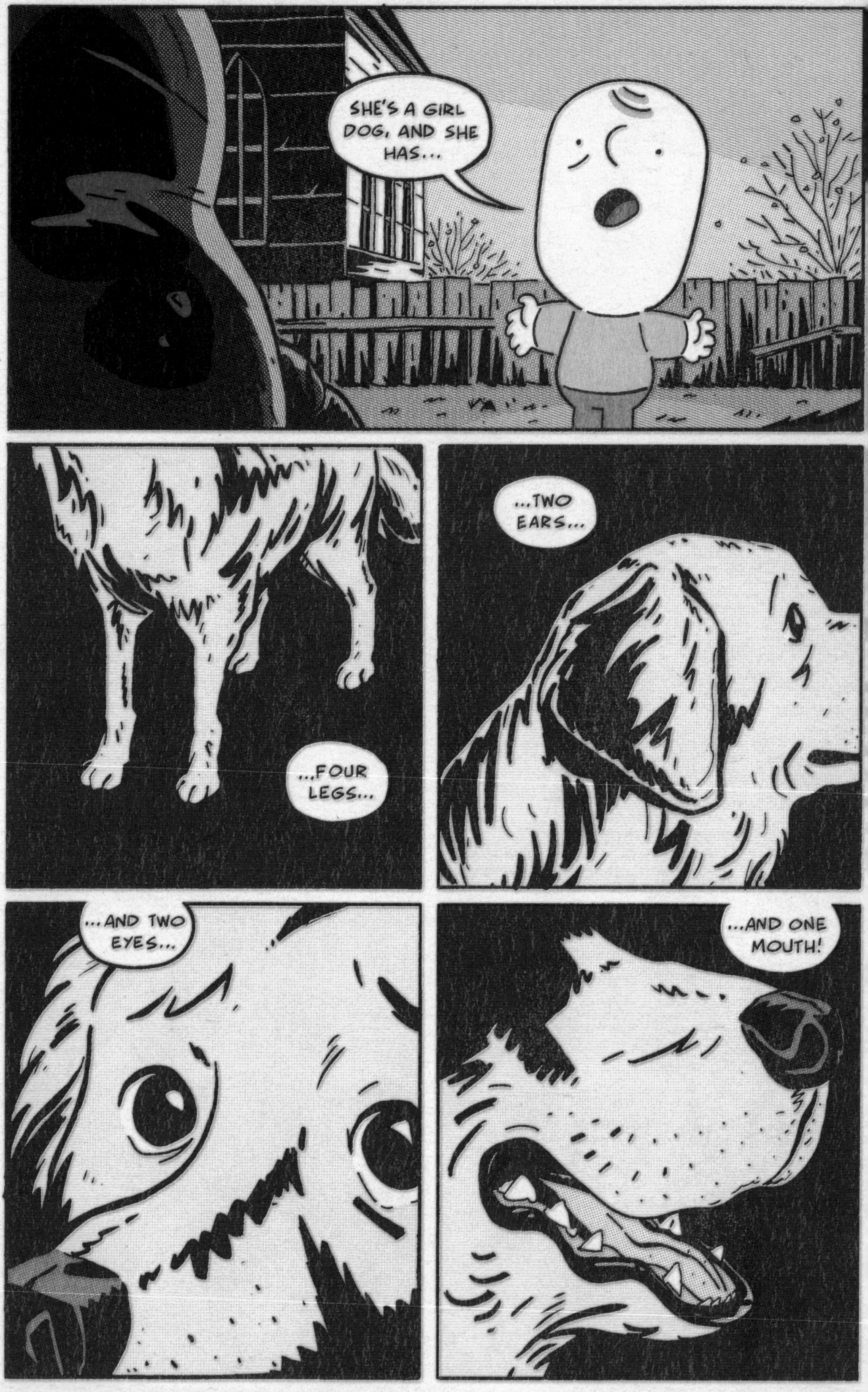
SHE'S A GIRL DOG, AND SHE HAS...
...FOUR LEGS...
...TWO EARS...
...AND TWO EYES...
...AND ONE MOUTH!

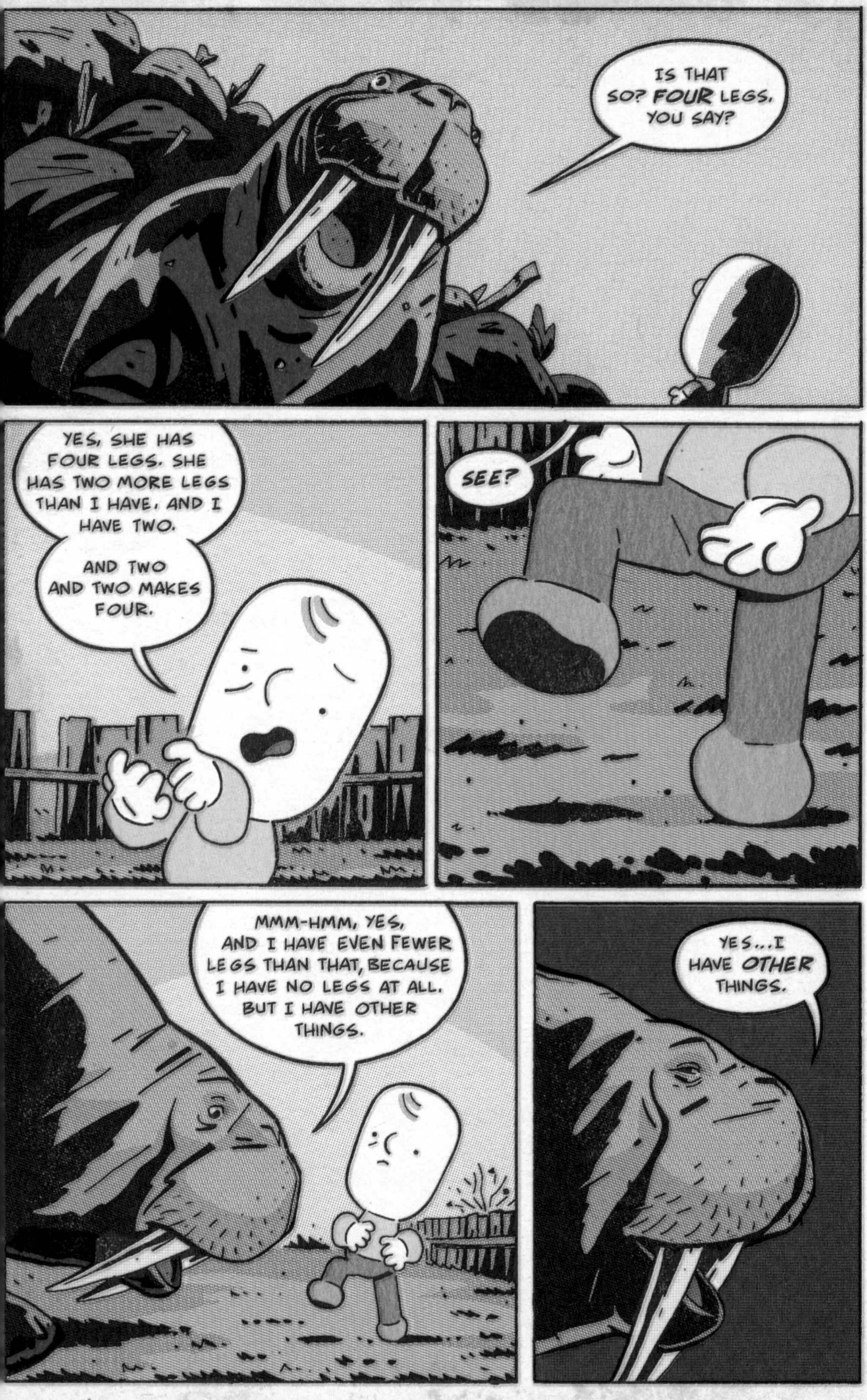
IS THAT SO? FOUR LEGS, YOU SAY?
YES, SHE HAS FOUR LEGS. SHE HAS TWO MORE LEGS THAN I HAVE, AND I HAVE TWO.
AND TWO AND TWO MAKES FOUR.
SEE?
MMM-HMM, YES, AND I HAVE EVEN FEWER LEGS THAN THAT, BECAUSE I HAVE NO LEGS AT ALL. BUT I HAVE OTHER THINGS.
YES...I HAVE OTHER THINGS.

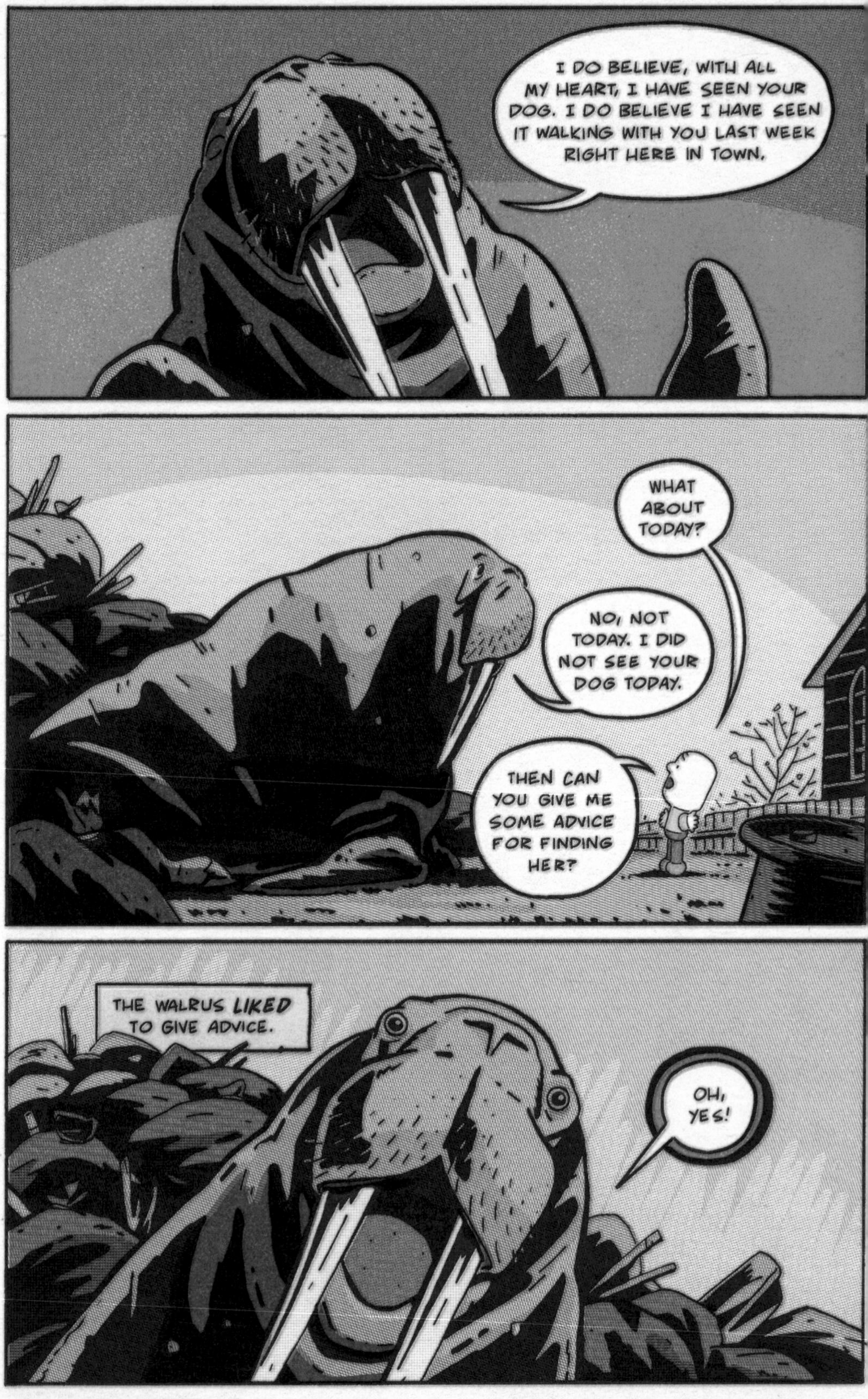
I DO BELIEVE, WITH ALL MY HEART, I HAVE SEEN YOUR DOG. I DO BELIEVE I HAVE SEEN IT WALKING WITH YOU LAST WEEK RIGHT HERE IN TOWN.
WHAT ABOUT TODAY?
NO, NOT TODAY. I DID NOT SEE YOUR DOG TODAY.
THEN CAN YOU GIVE ME SOME ADVICE FOR FINDING HER?
THE WALRUS *LIKED* TO GIVE ADVICE.
OH, YES!

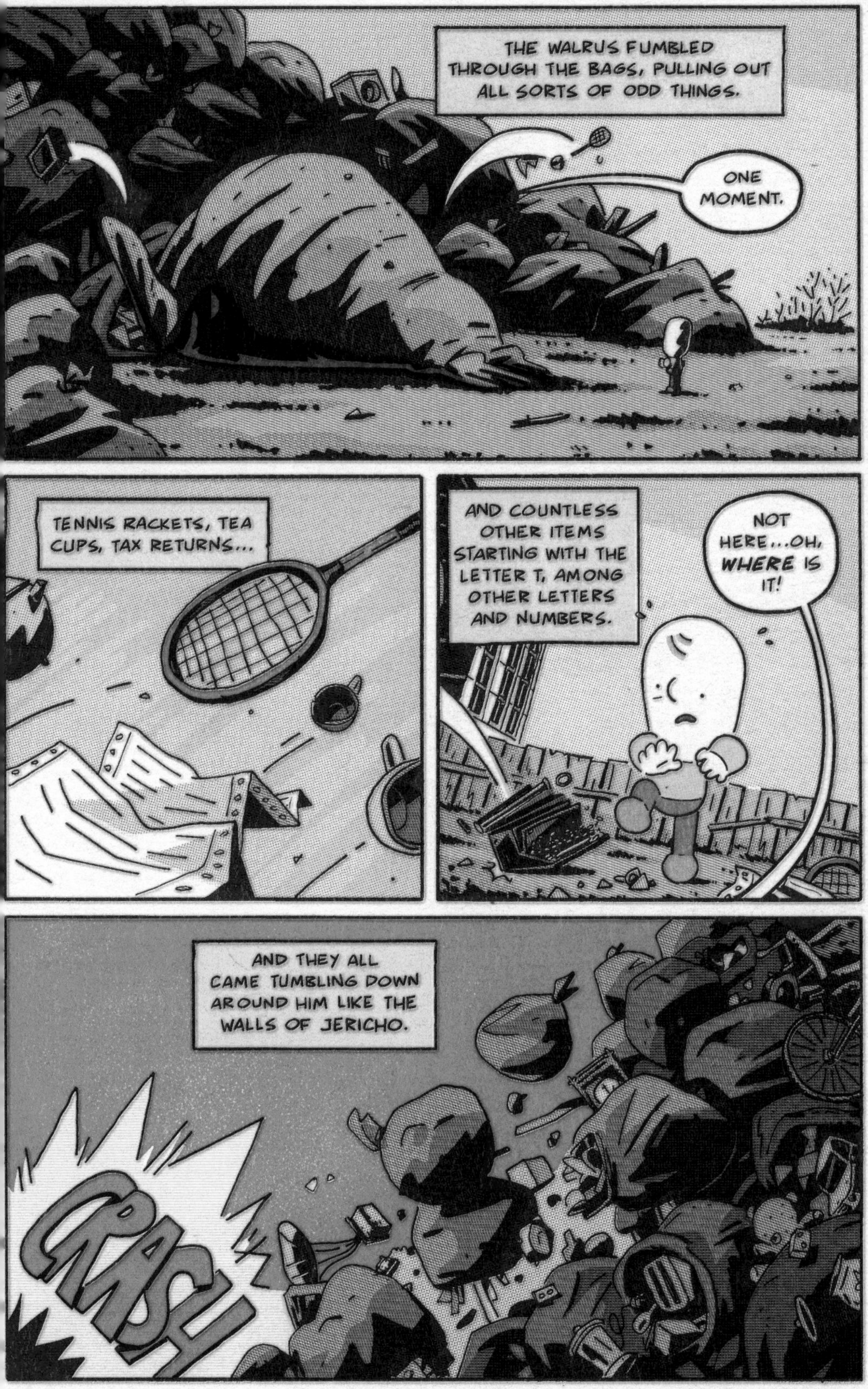
THE WALRUS FUMBLED THROUGH THE BAGS, PULLING OUT ALL SORTS OF ODD THINGS.
ONE MOMENT.
TENNIS RACKETS, TEA CUPS, TAX RETURNS...
AND COUNTLESS OTHER ITEMS STARTING WITH THE LETTER T, AMONG OTHER LETTERS AND NUMBERS.
NOT HERE...OH, WHERE IS IT!
AND THEY ALL CAME TUMBLING DOWN AROUND HIM LIKE THE WALLS OF JERICHO.
CRASH

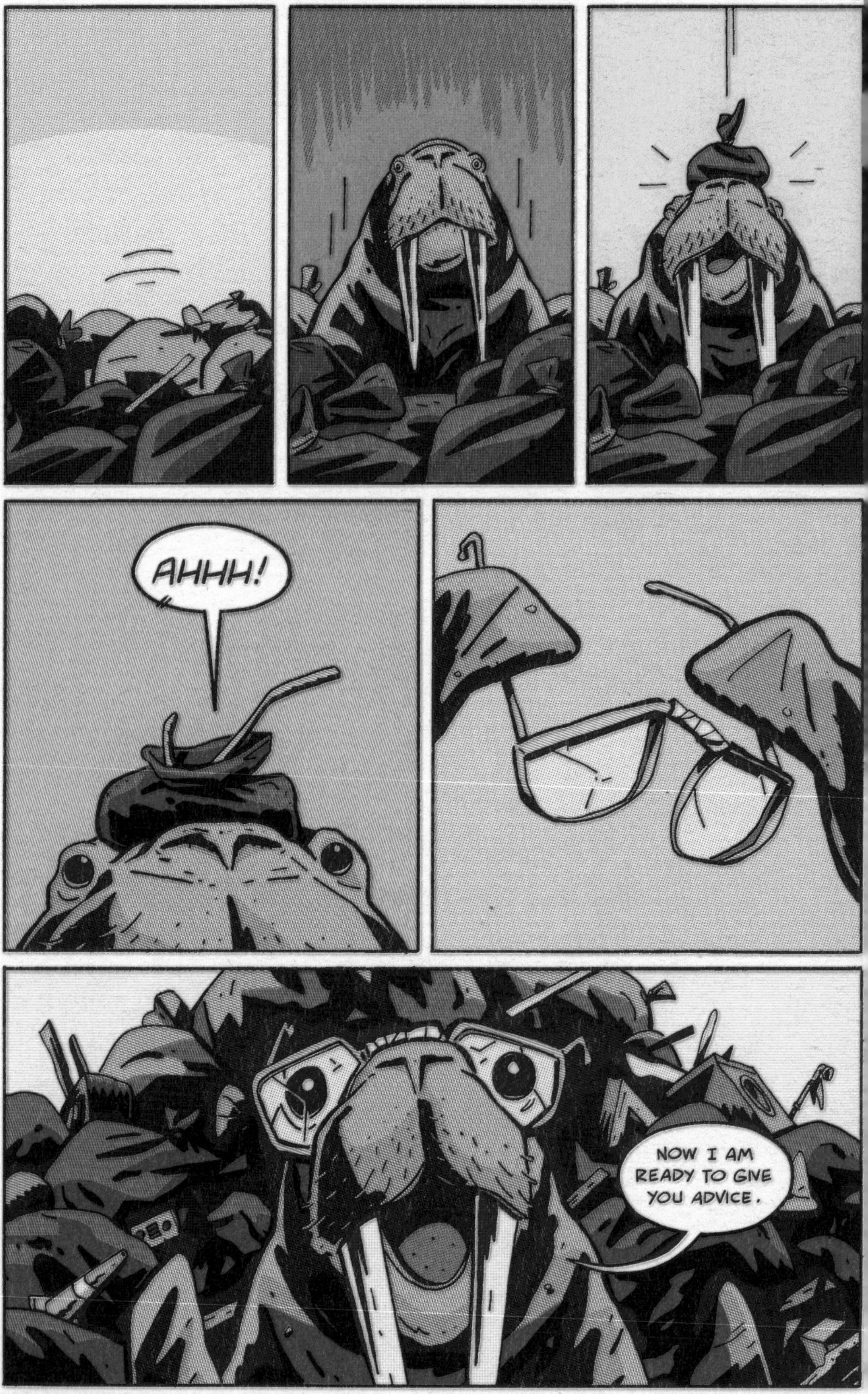
AHHH!
NOW I AM READY TO GIVE YOU ADVICE.

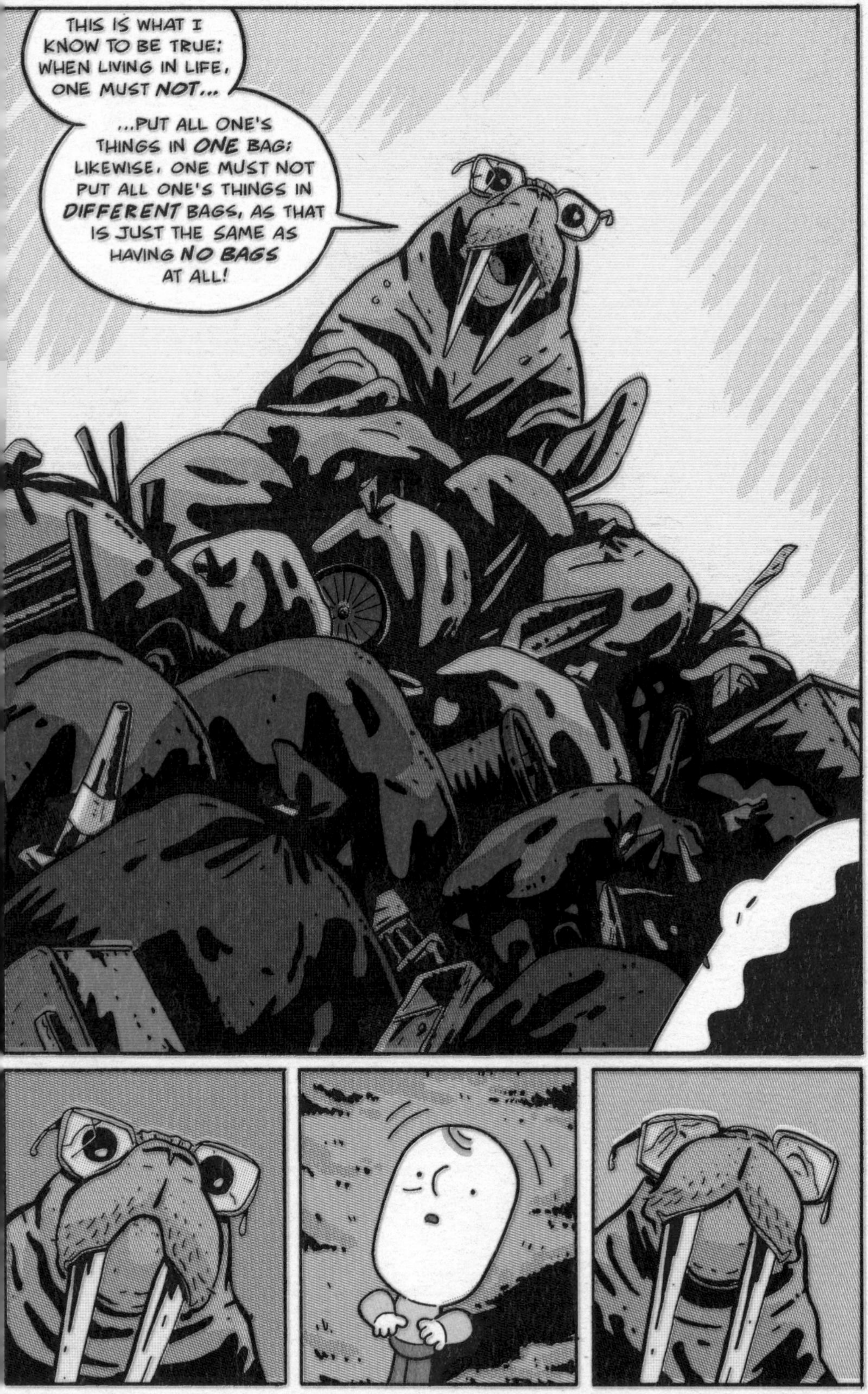
THIS IS WHAT I KNOW TO BE TRUE: WHEN LIVING IN LIFE, ONE MUST NOT...
...PUT ALL ONE'S THINGS IN ONE BAG; LIKEWISE, ONE MUST NOT PUT ALL ONE'S THINGS IN DIFFERENT BAGS, AS THAT IS JUST THE SAME AS HAVING NO BAGS AT ALL!

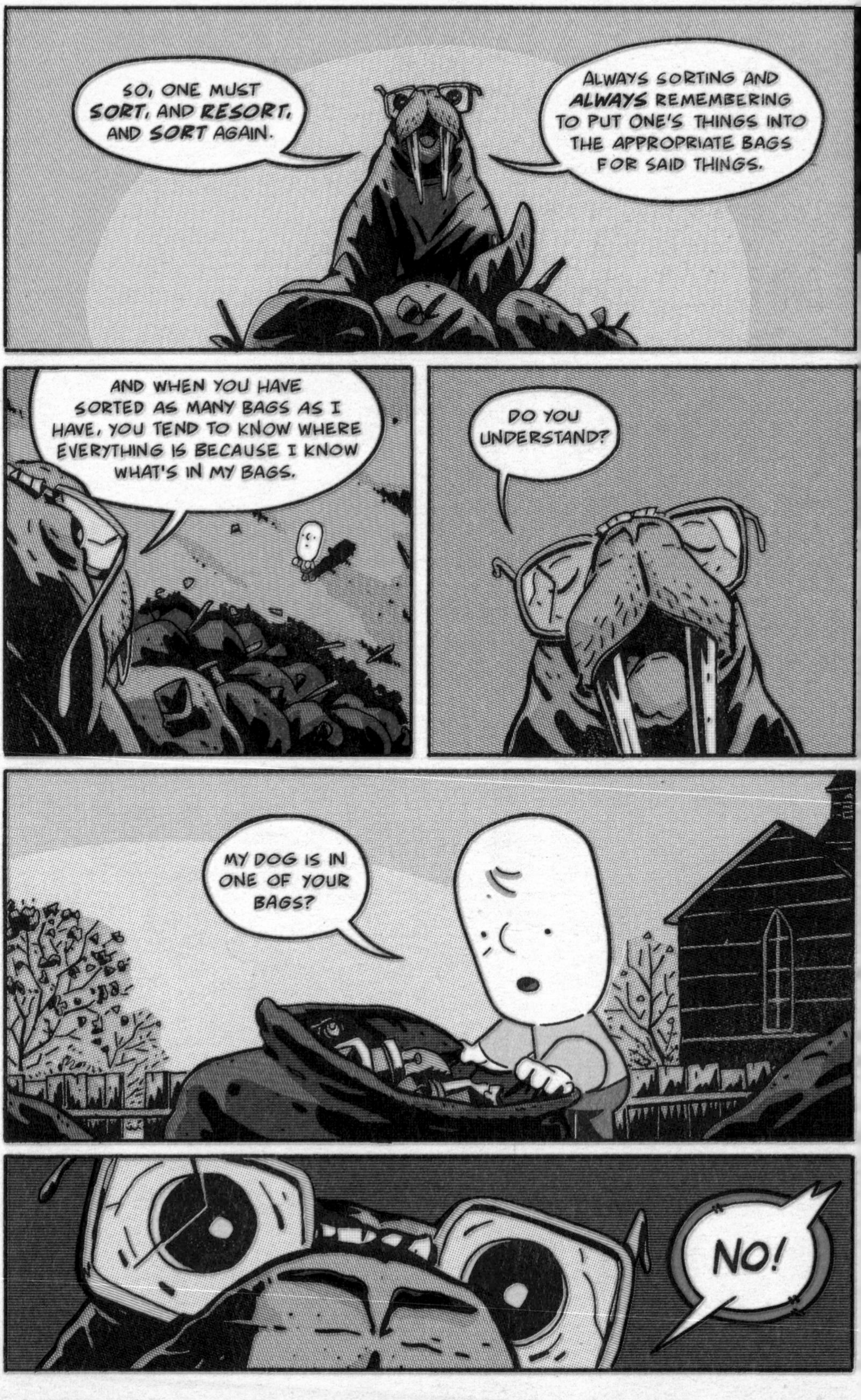
SO, ONE MUST SORT, AND RESORT, AND SORT AGAIN.
ALWAYS SORTING AND ALWAYS REMEMBERING TO PUT ONE'S THINGS INTO THE APPROPRIATE BAGS FOR SAID THINGS.
AND WHEN YOU HAVE SORTED AS MANY BAGS AS I HAVE, YOU TEND TO KNOW WHERE EVERYTHING IS BECAUSE I KNOW WHAT'S IN MY BAGS.
DO YOU UNDERSTAND?
MY DOG IS IN ONE OF YOUR BAGS?
NO!

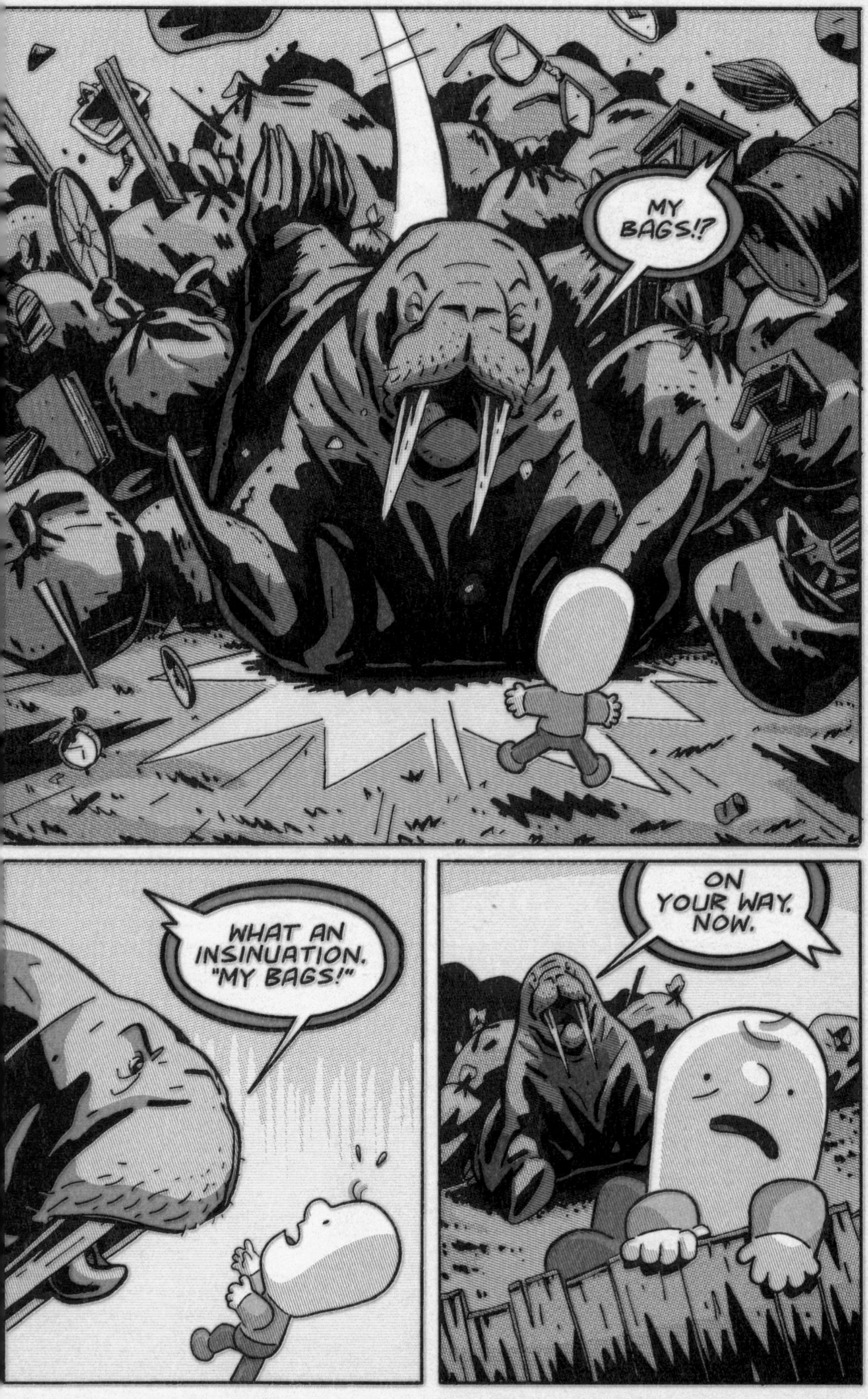
MY BAGS!?
WHAT AN INSINUATION. "MY BAGS!"
ON YOUR WAY. NOW.

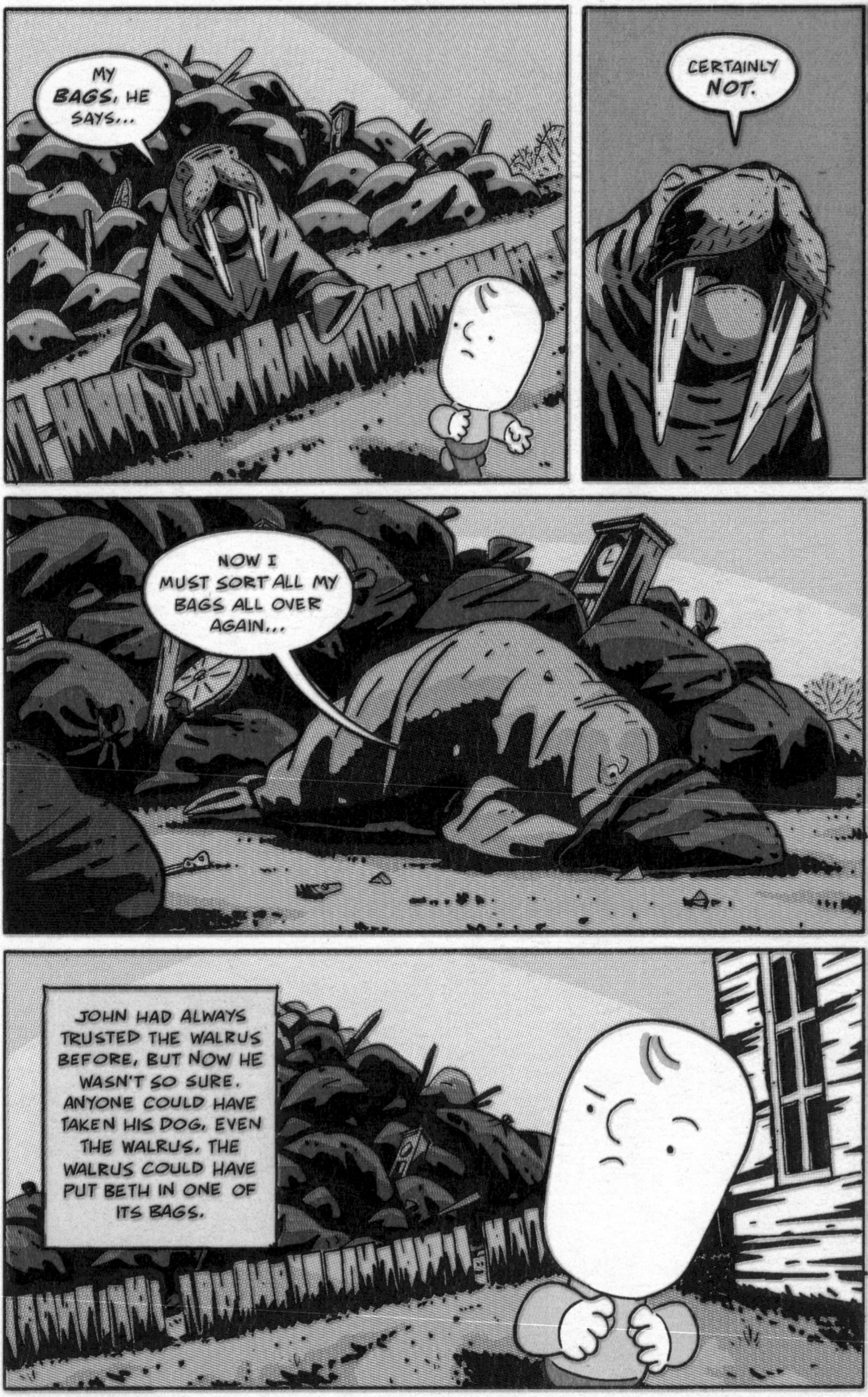
MY BAGS, HE SAYS...
CERTAINLY NOT.
NOW I MUST SORT ALL MY BAGS ALL OVER AGAIN...
JOHN HAD ALWAYS TRUSTED THE WALRUS BEFORE, BUT NOW HE WASN'T SO SURE. ANYONE COULD HAVE TAKEN HIS DOG, EVEN THE WALRUS. THE WALRUS COULD HAVE PUT BETH IN ONE OF ITS BAGS.

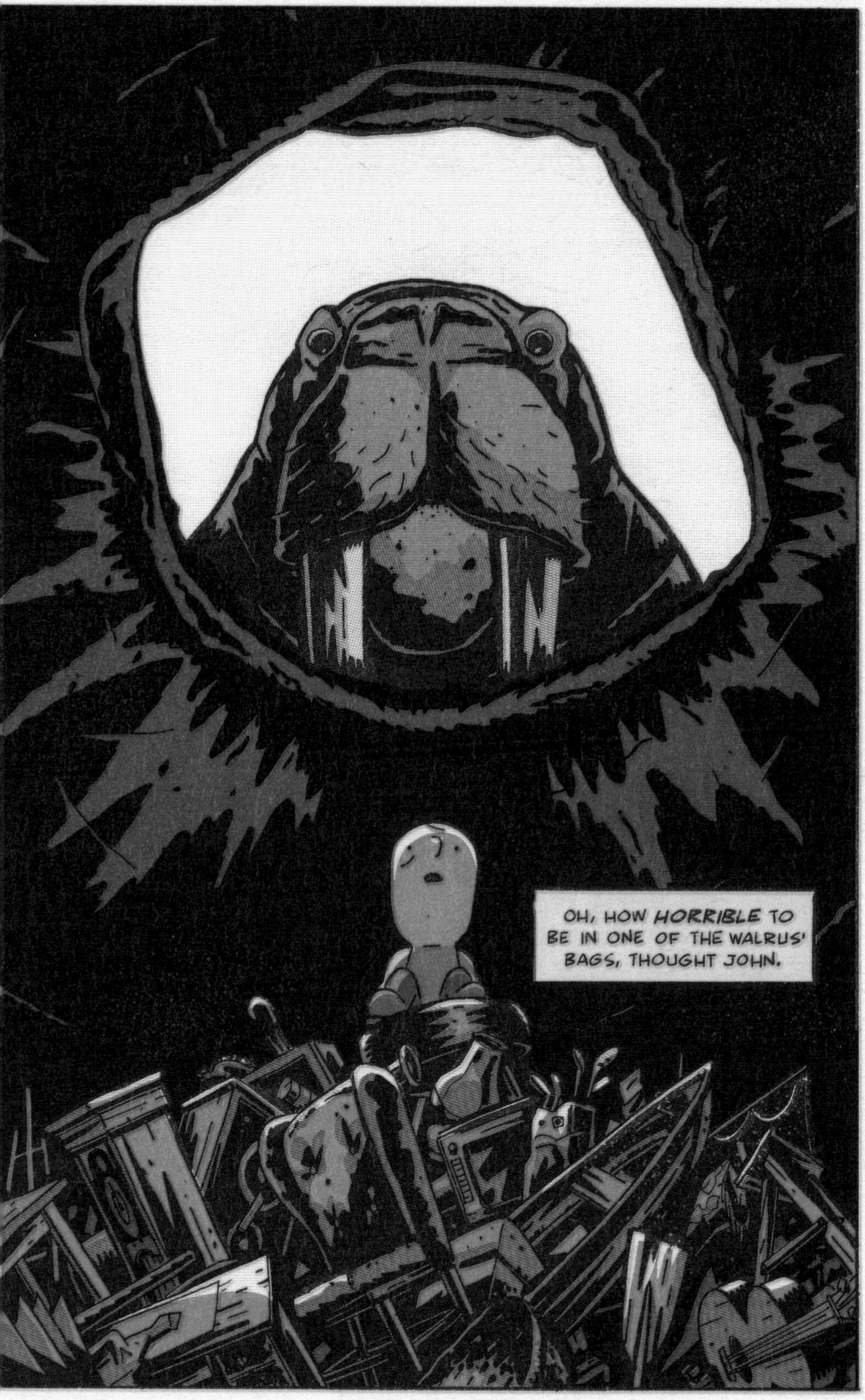
OH, HOW HORRIBLE TO BE IN ONE OF THE WALRUS' BAGS, THOUGHT JOHN.

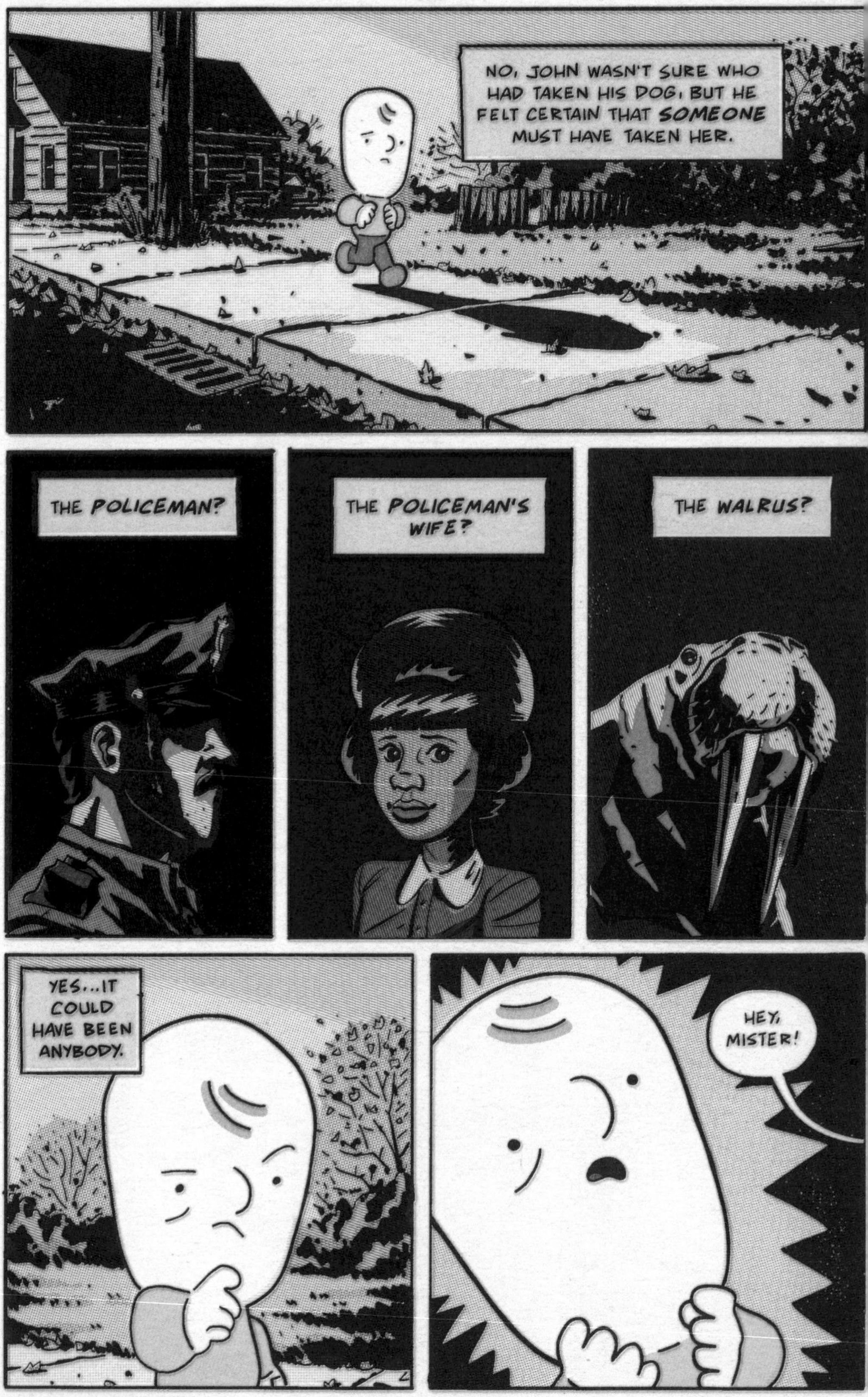
NO, JOHN WASN'T SURE WHO HAD TAKEN HIS DOG, BUT HE FELT CERTAIN THAT SOMEONE MUST HAVE TAKEN HER.
THE POLICEMAN?
THE POLICEMAN'S WIFE?
THE WALRUS?
YES...IT COULD HAVE BEEN ANYBODY.
HEY, MISTER!

JOHN SAW TWO BOYS PLAYING WITH JACKS ON THE SIDEWALK. THEY SEEMED LIKE TOUGH BOYS.

ONE OF THEM WAS WEARING A BLUE HAT; THE OTHER ONE WAS WEARING A YELLOW CAT.

SCREE!

I KNOW WHO YOU ARE.

ME?

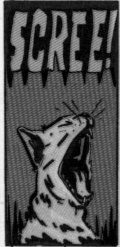

SCREE!

YEAH, MISTER, YOU'RE THE ONE WHO GOT A DOG, RIGHT?

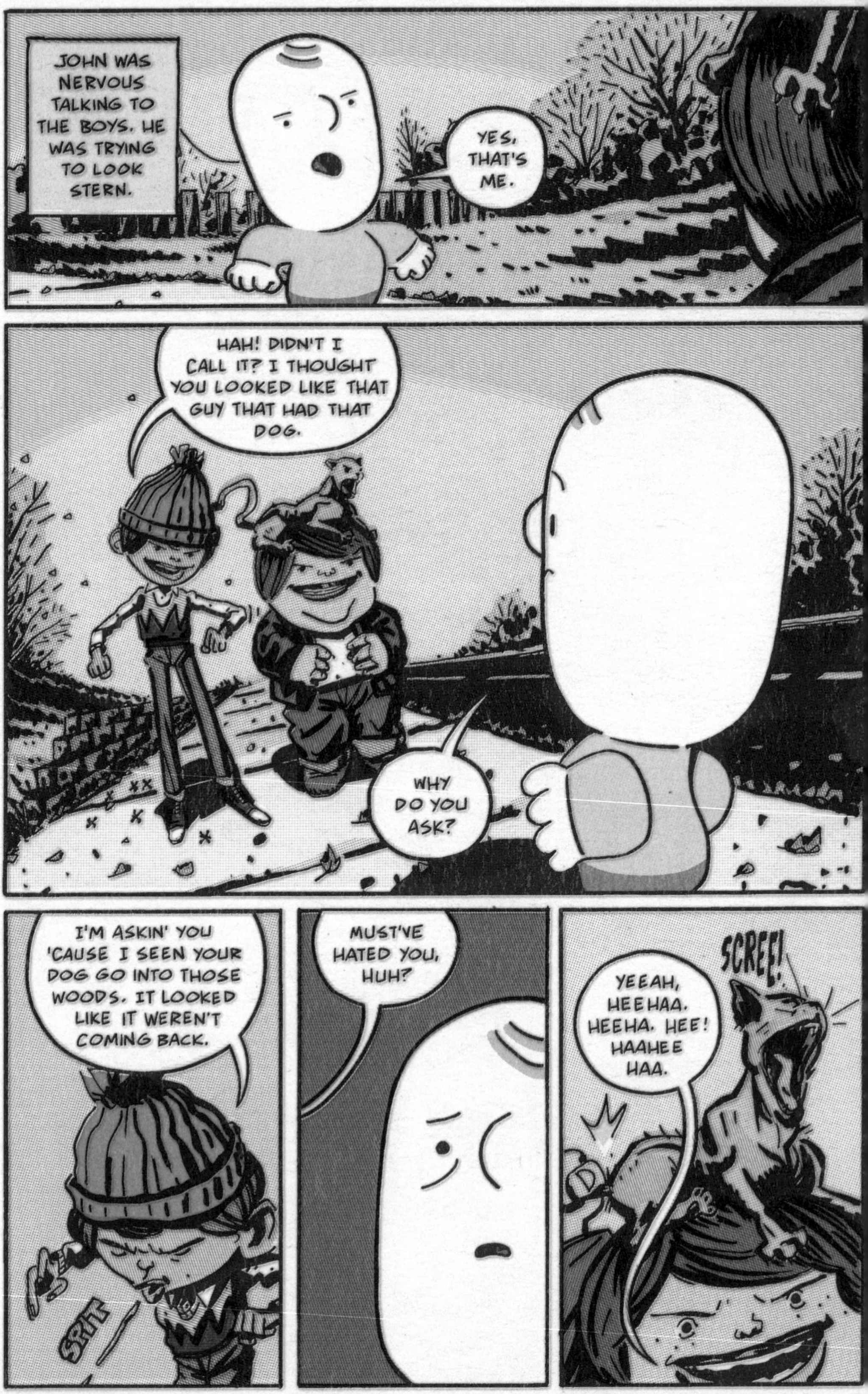
JOHN WAS NERVOUS TALKING TO THE BOYS. HE WAS TRYING TO LOOK STERN.
YES, THAT'S ME.
HAH! DIDN'T I CALL IT? I THOUGHT YOU LOOKED LIKE THAT GUY THAT HAD THAT DOG.
WHY DO YOU ASK?
I'M ASKIN' YOU 'CAUSE I SEEN YOUR DOG GO INTO THOSE WOODS. IT LOOKED LIKE IT WEREN'T COMING BACK.
SPIT
MUST'VE HATED YOU, HUH?
SCREE!
YEEAH, HEEHAA. HEEHA. HEE! HAAHEE HAA.

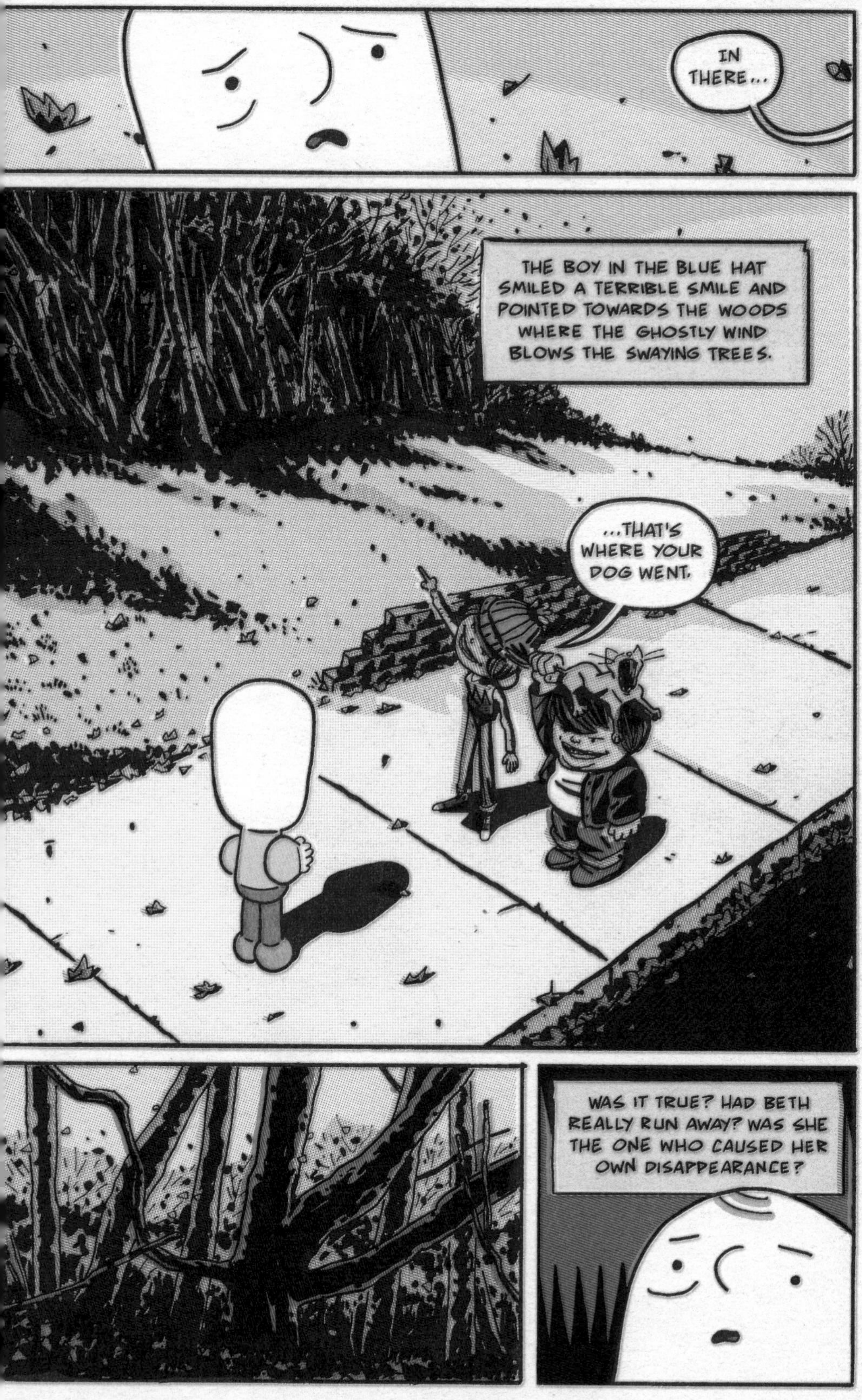
IN THERE...
THE BOY IN THE BLUE HAT SMILED A TERRIBLE SMILE AND POINTED TOWARDS THE WOODS WHERE THE GHOSTLY WIND BLOWS THE SWAYING TREES.
...THAT'S WHERE YOUR DOG WENT.
WAS IT TRUE? HAD BETH REALLY RUN AWAY? WAS SHE THE ONE WHO CAUSED HER OWN DISAPPEARANCE?

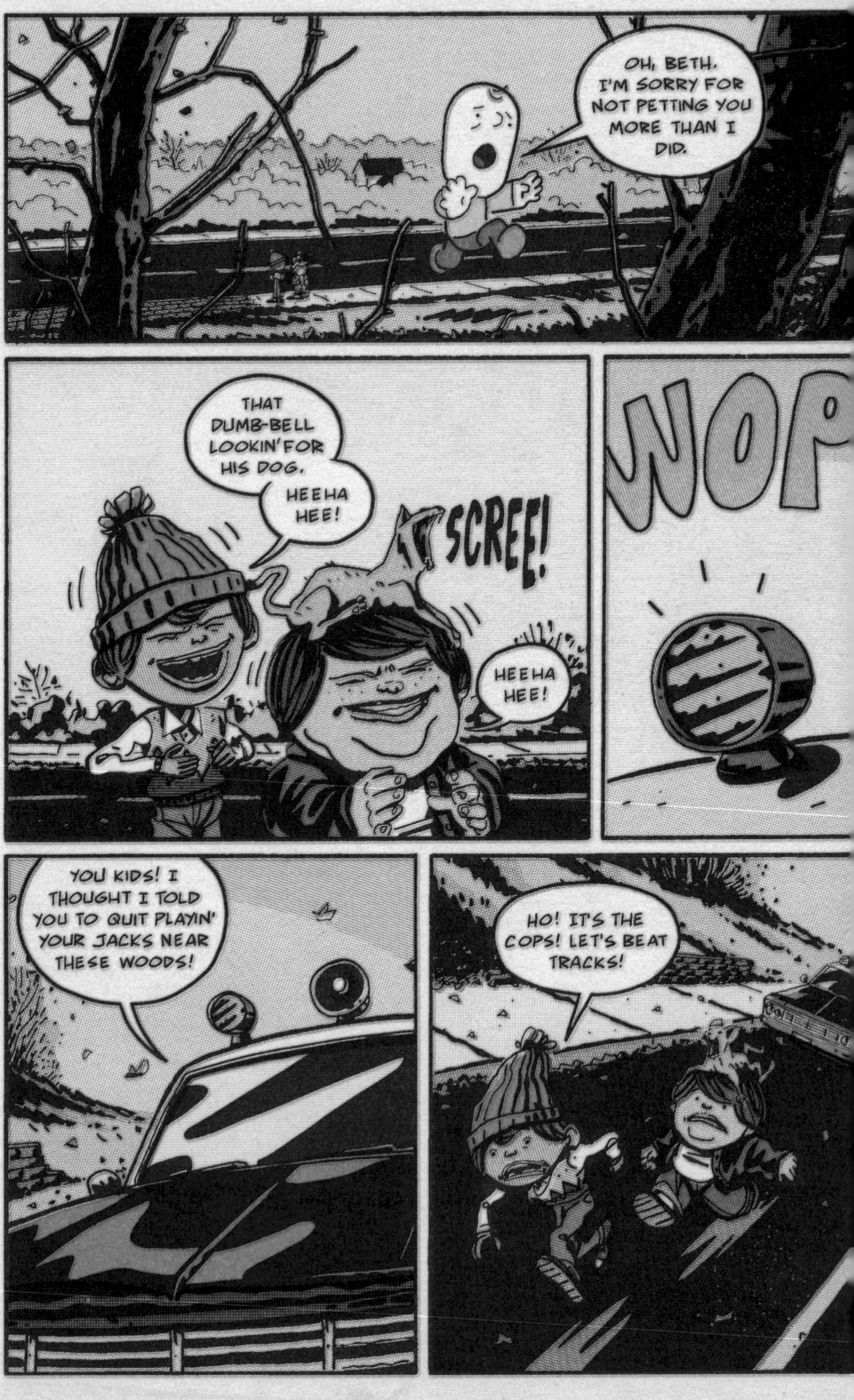
OH, BETH. I'M SORRY FOR NOT PETTING YOU MORE THAN I DID.
THAT DUMB-BELL LOOKIN' FOR HIS DOG.
HEEHA HEE!
SCREE!
HEEHA HEE!
WOP
YOU KIDS! I THOUGHT I TOLD YOU TO QUIT PLAYIN' YOUR JACKS NEAR THESE WOODS!
HO! IT'S THE COPS! LET'S BEAT TRACKS!

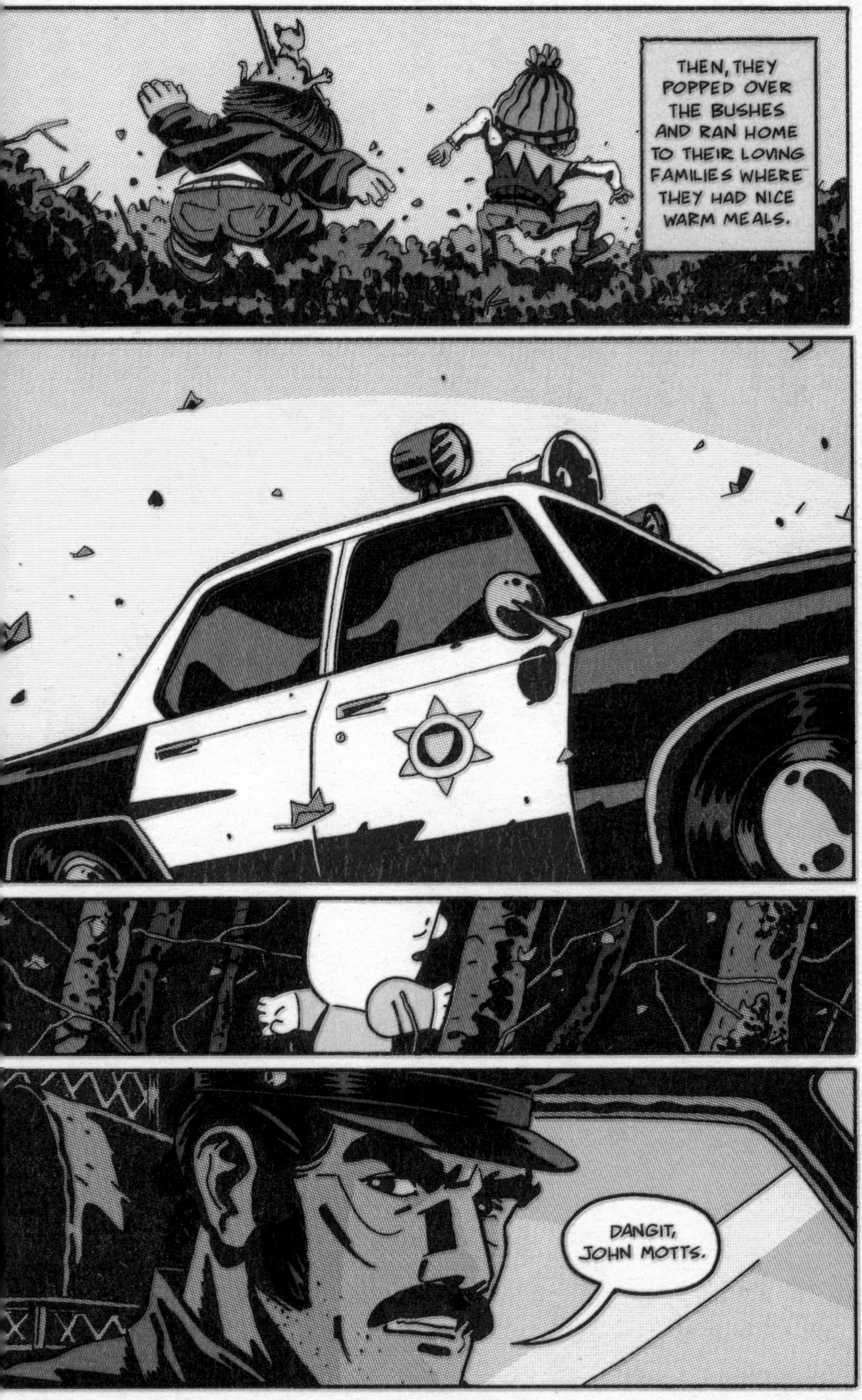
THEN, THEY POPPED OVER THE BUSHES AND RAN HOME TO THEIR LOVING FAMILIES WHERE THEY HAD NICE WARM MEALS.
DANGIT, JOHN MOTTS.

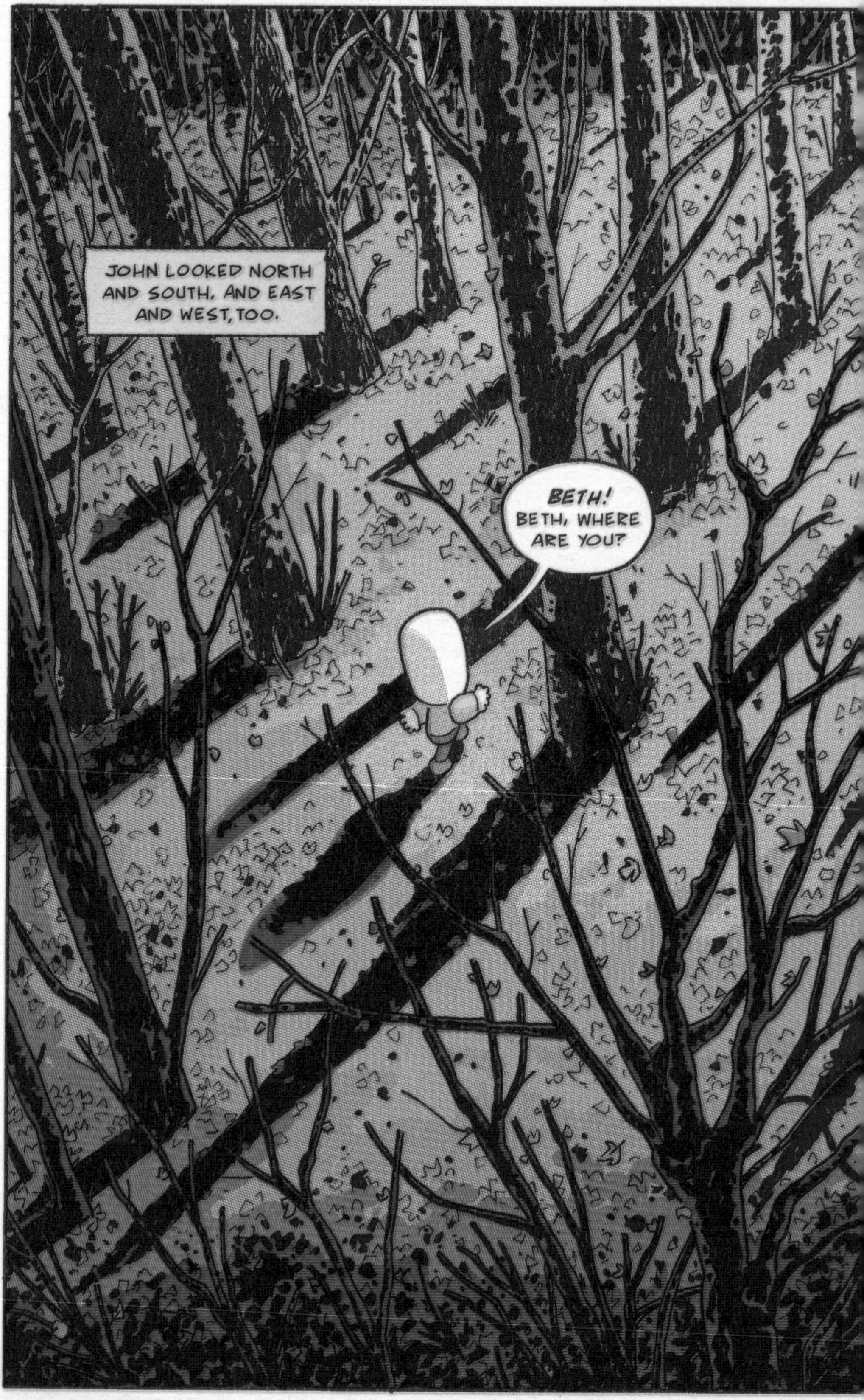
JOHN LOOKED NORTH AND SOUTH, AND EAST AND WEST, TOO.
BETH! BETH, WHERE ARE YOU?

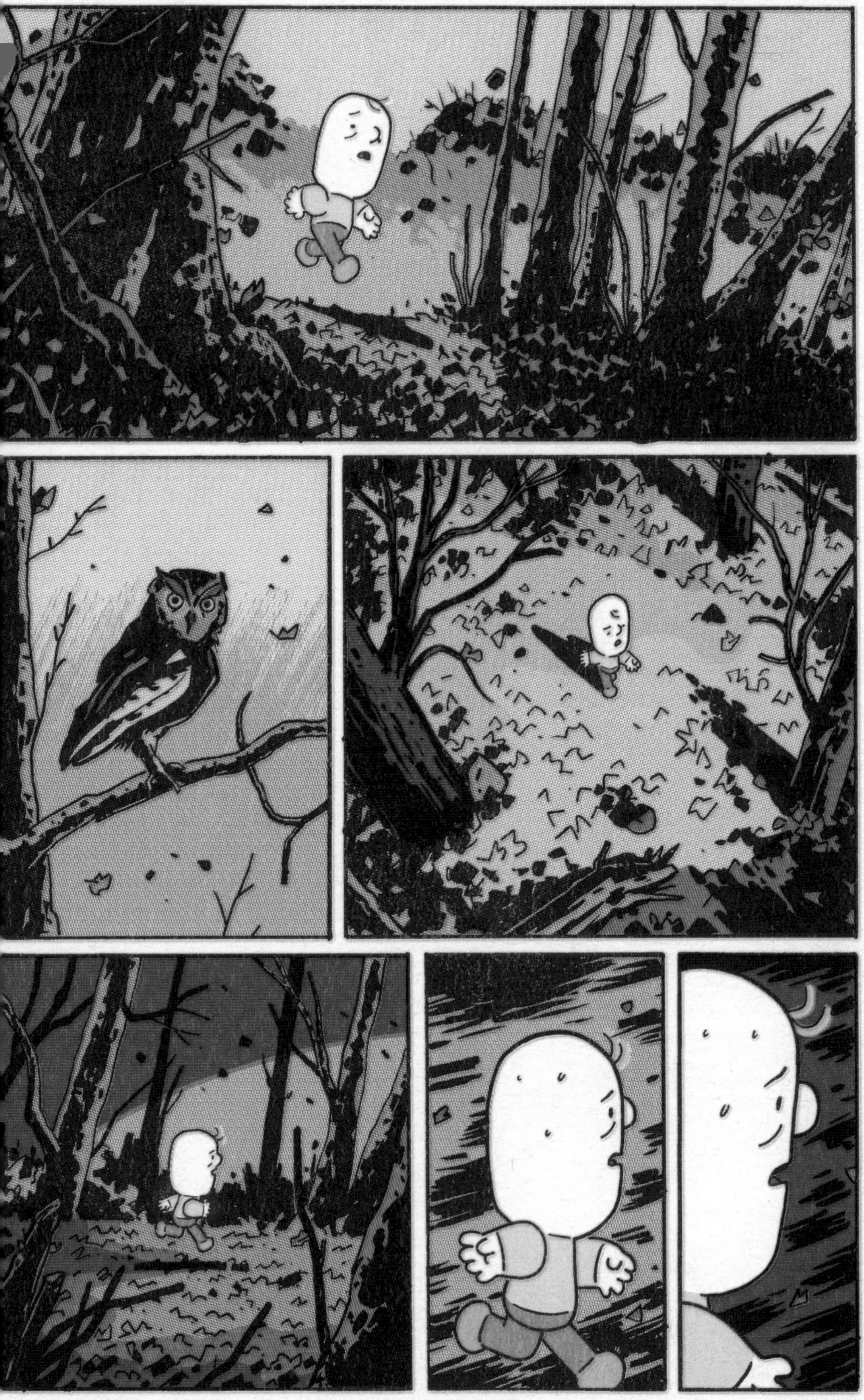

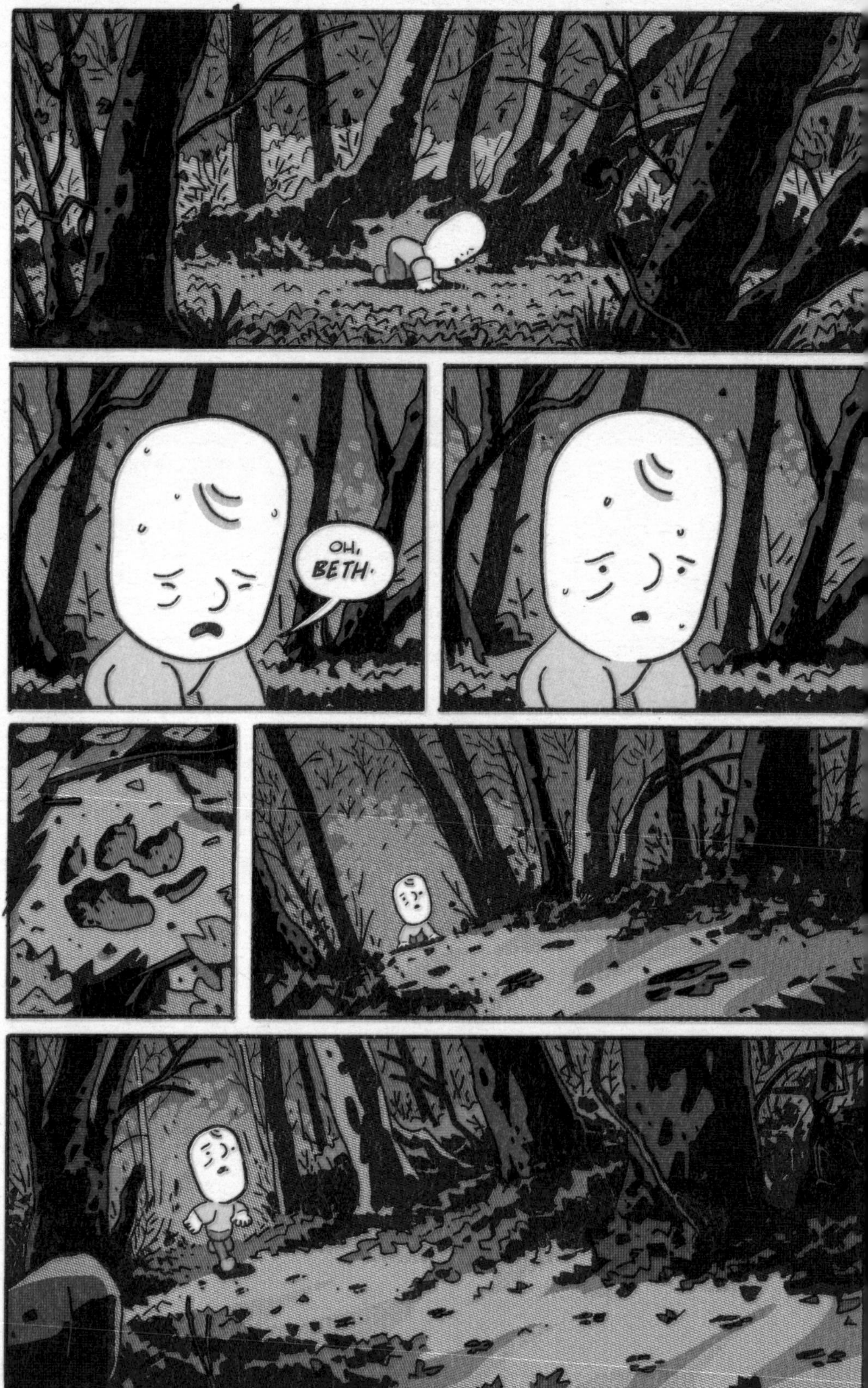
OH, BETH.

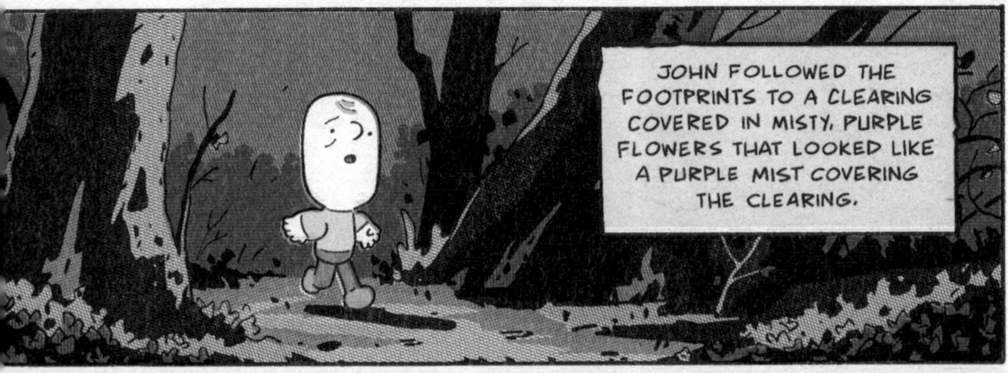
JOHN FOLLOWED THE FOOTPRINTS TO A CLEARING COVERED IN MISTY, PURPLE FLOWERS THAT LOOKED LIKE A PURPLE MIST COVERING THE CLEARING.

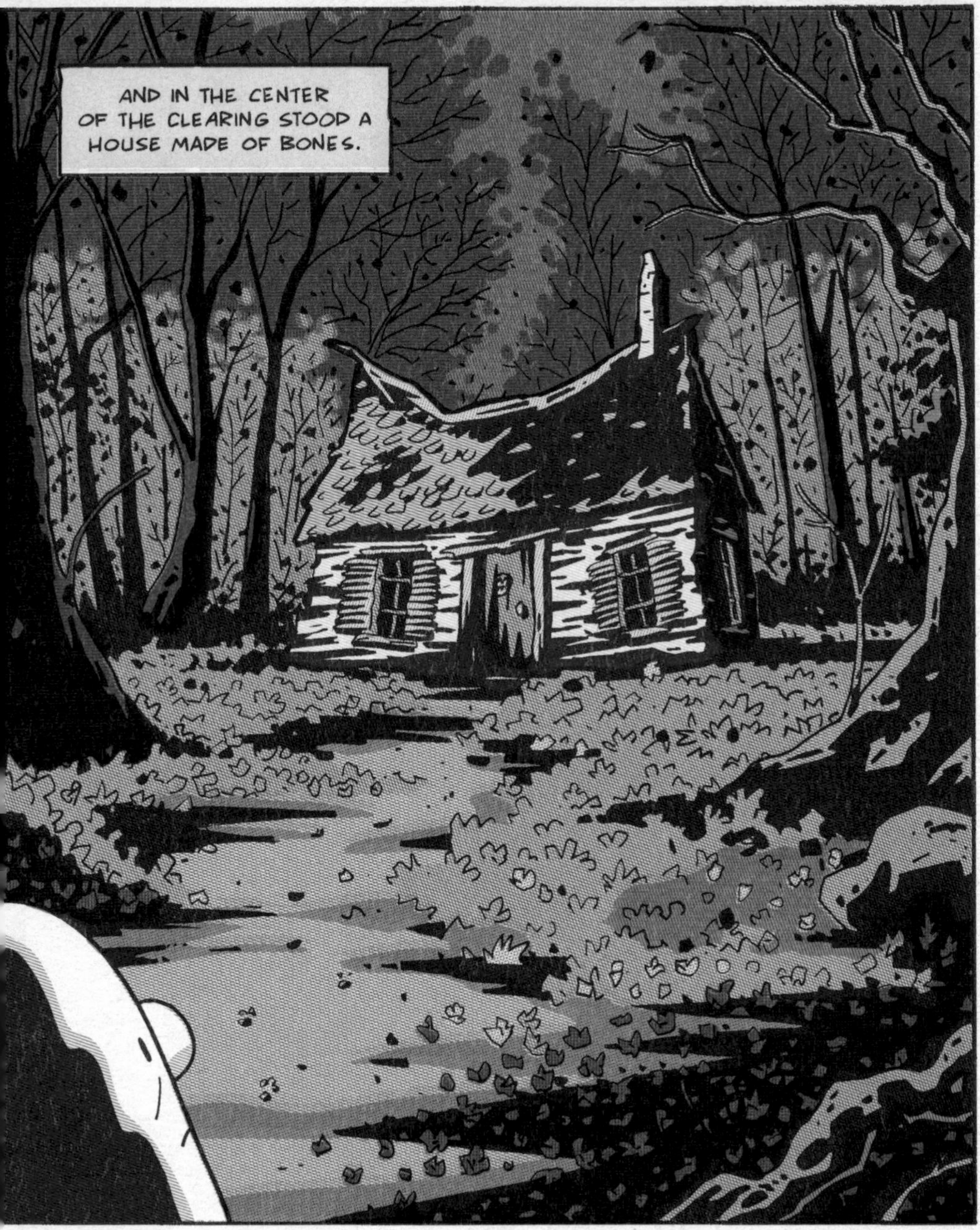
AND IN THE CENTER OF THE CLEARING STOOD A HOUSE MADE OF BONES.

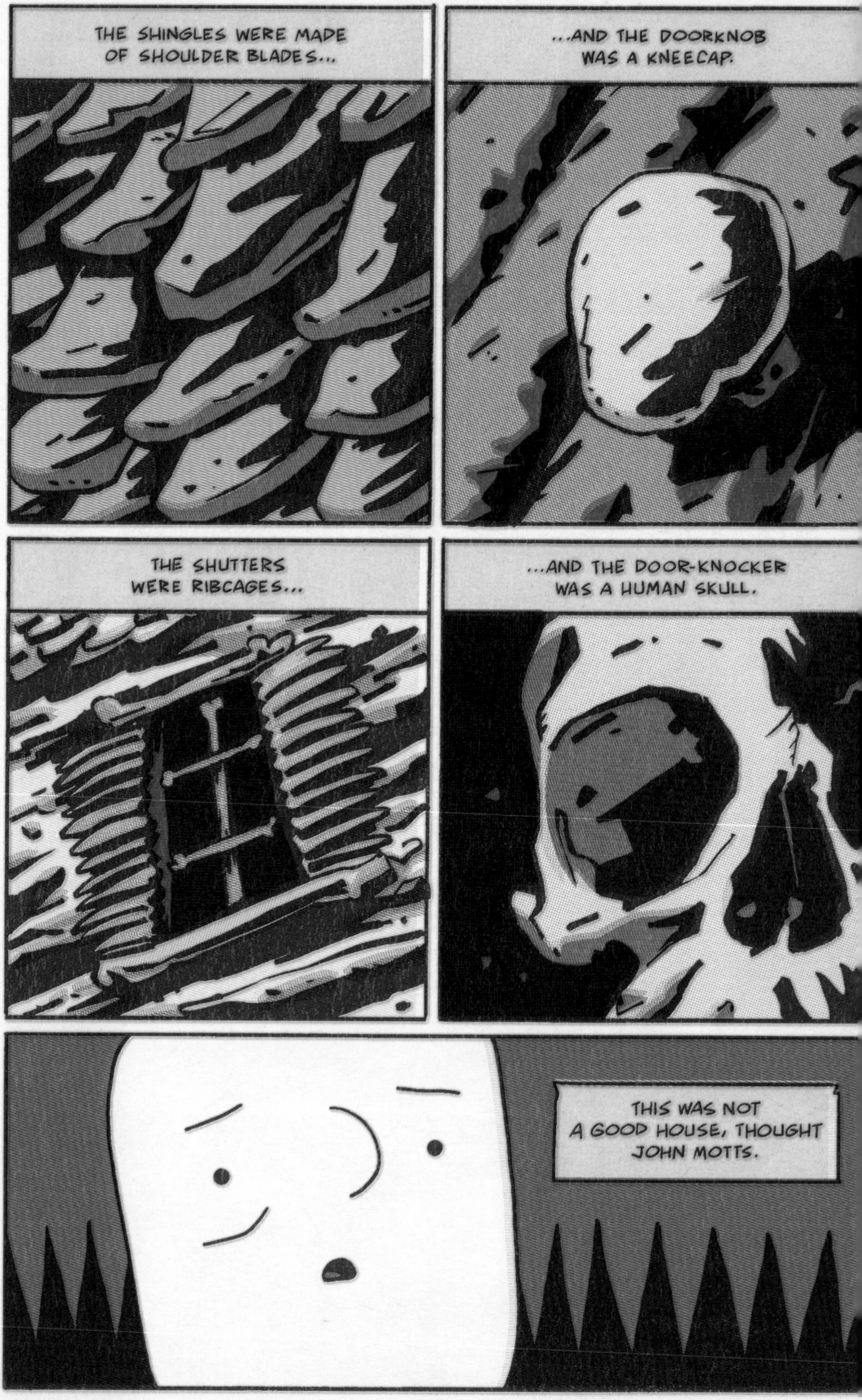
THE SHINGLES WERE MADE OF SHOULDER BLADES...
...AND THE DOORKNOB WAS A KNEECAP.
THE SHUTTERS WERE RIBCAGES...
...AND THE DOOR-KNOCKER WAS A HUMAN SKULL.
THIS WAS NOT A GOOD HOUSE, THOUGHT JOHN MOTTS.

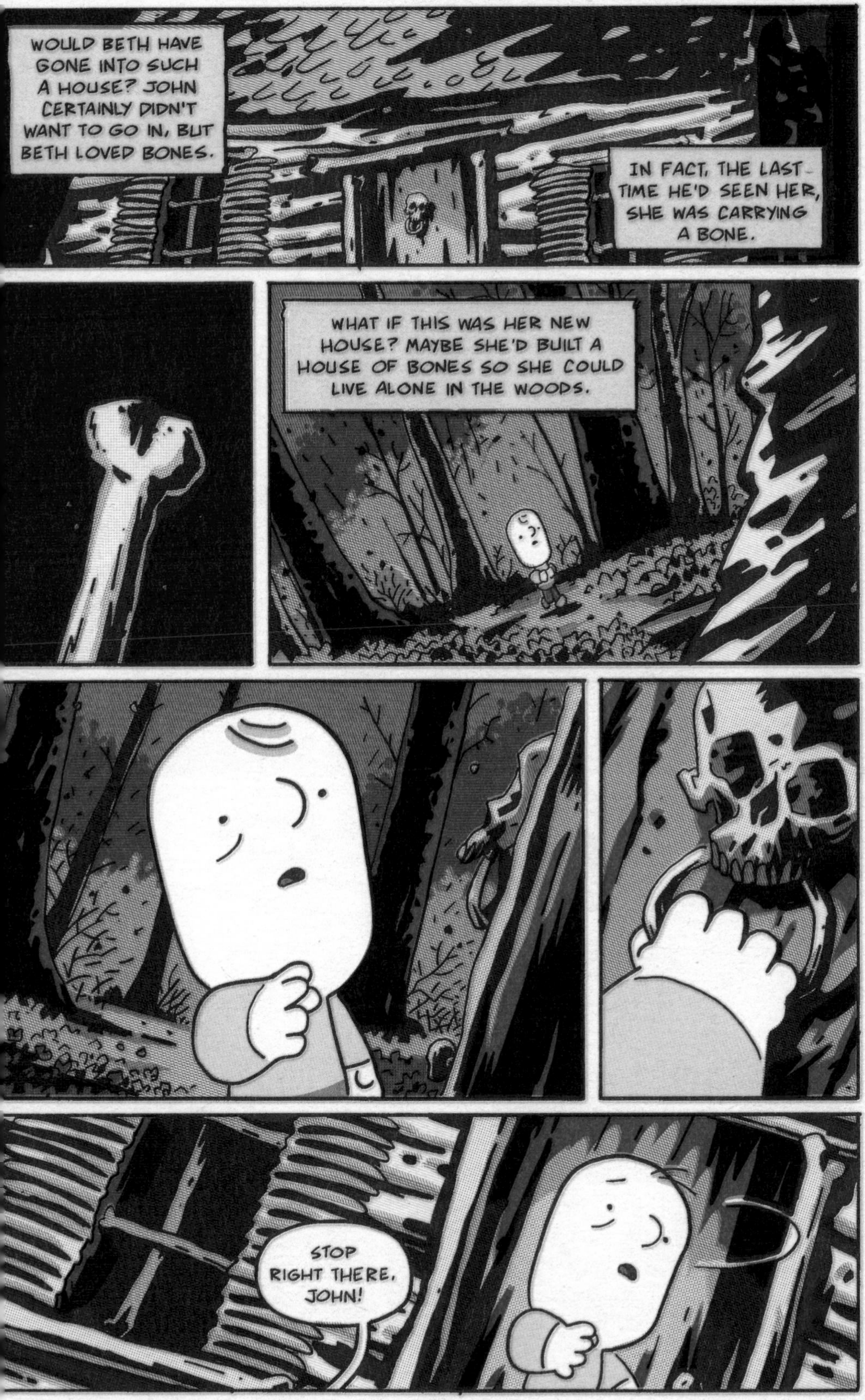
WOULD BETH HAVE GONE INTO SUCH A HOUSE? JOHN CERTAINLY DIDN'T WANT TO GO IN, BUT BETH LOVED BONES.
IN FACT, THE LAST TIME HE'D SEEN HER, SHE WAS CARRYING A BONE.
WHAT IF THIS WAS HER NEW HOUSE? MAYBE SHE'D BUILT A HOUSE OF BONES SO SHE COULD LIVE ALONE IN THE WOODS.
STOP RIGHT THERE, JOHN!

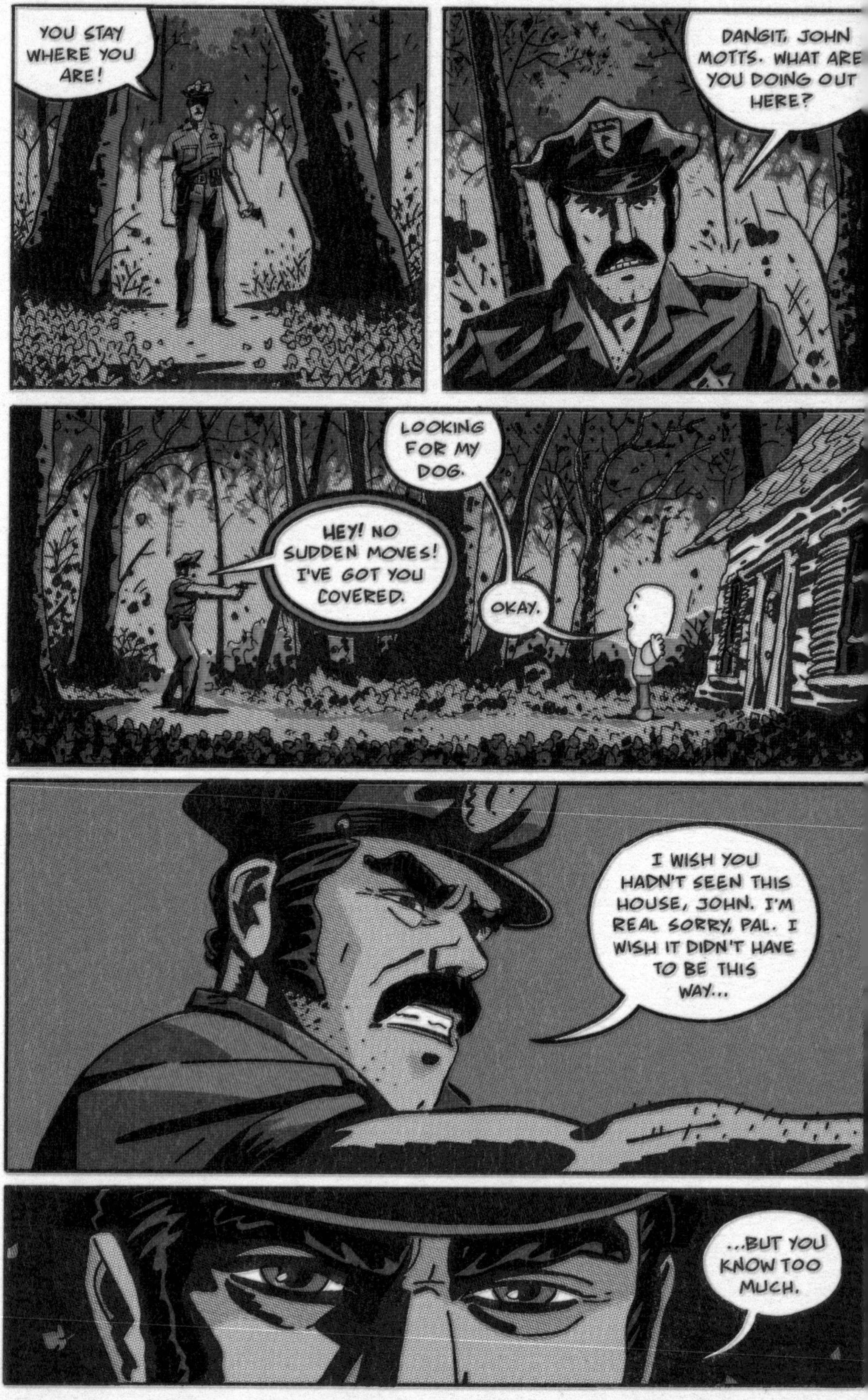
YOU STAY WHERE YOU ARE!
DANGIT, JOHN MOTTS. WHAT ARE YOU DOING OUT HERE?
LOOKING FOR MY DOG.
HEY! NO SUDDEN MOVES! I'VE GOT YOU COVERED.
OKAY.
I WISH YOU HADN'T SEEN THIS HOUSE, JOHN. I'M REAL SORRY, PAL. I WISH IT DIDN'T HAVE TO BE THIS WAY...
...BUT YOU KNOW TOO MUCH.

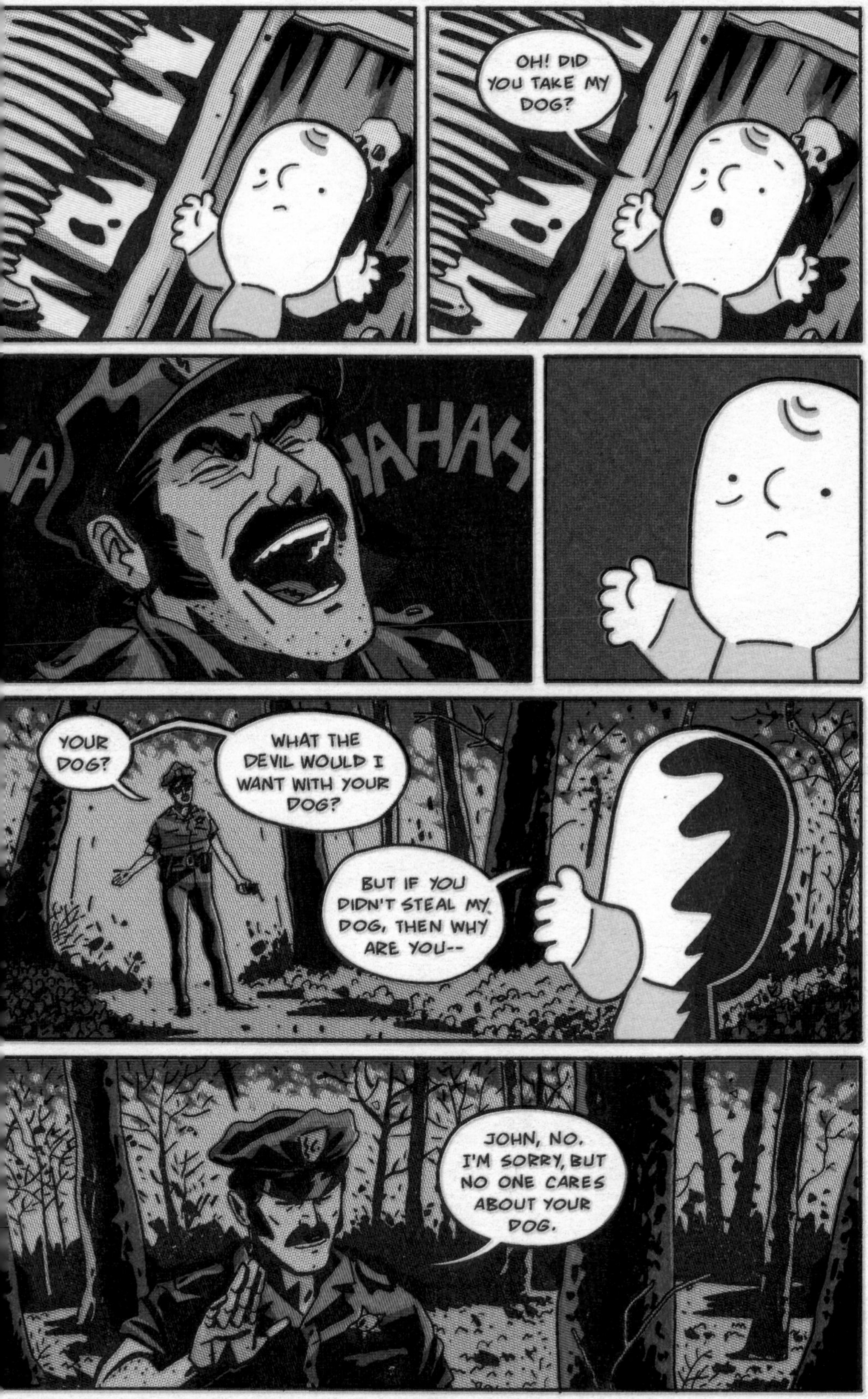
OH! DID YOU TAKE MY DOG?
HAHAHA
YOUR DOG?
WHAT THE DEVIL WOULD I WANT WITH YOUR DOG?
BUT IF YOU DIDN'T STEAL MY DOG, THEN WHY ARE YOU--
JOHN, NO. I'M SORRY, BUT NO ONE CARES ABOUT YOUR DOG.

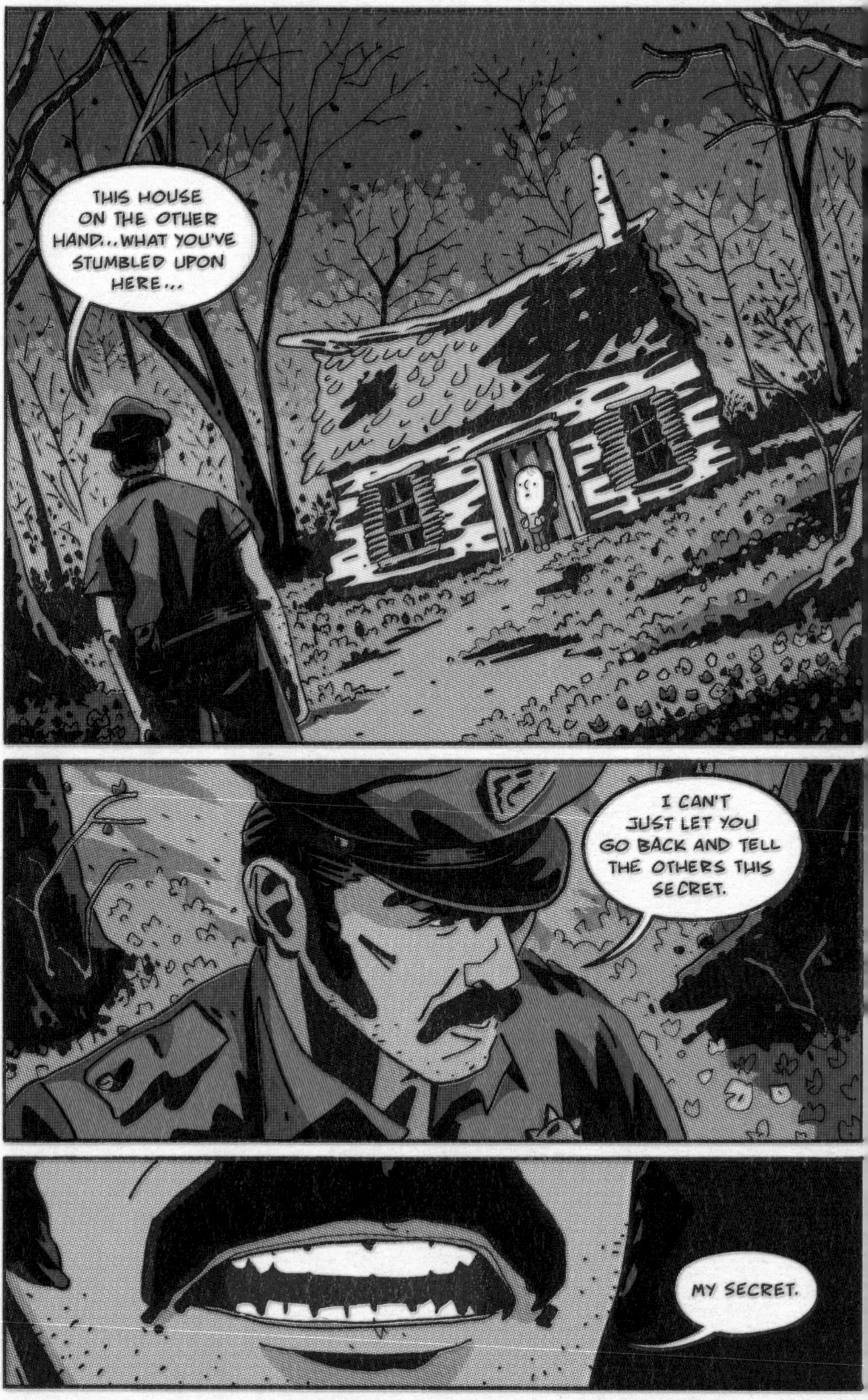
THIS HOUSE ON THE OTHER HAND...WHAT YOU'VE STUMBLED UPON HERE...
I CAN'T JUST LET YOU GO BACK AND TELL THE OTHERS THIS SECRET.
MY SECRET.

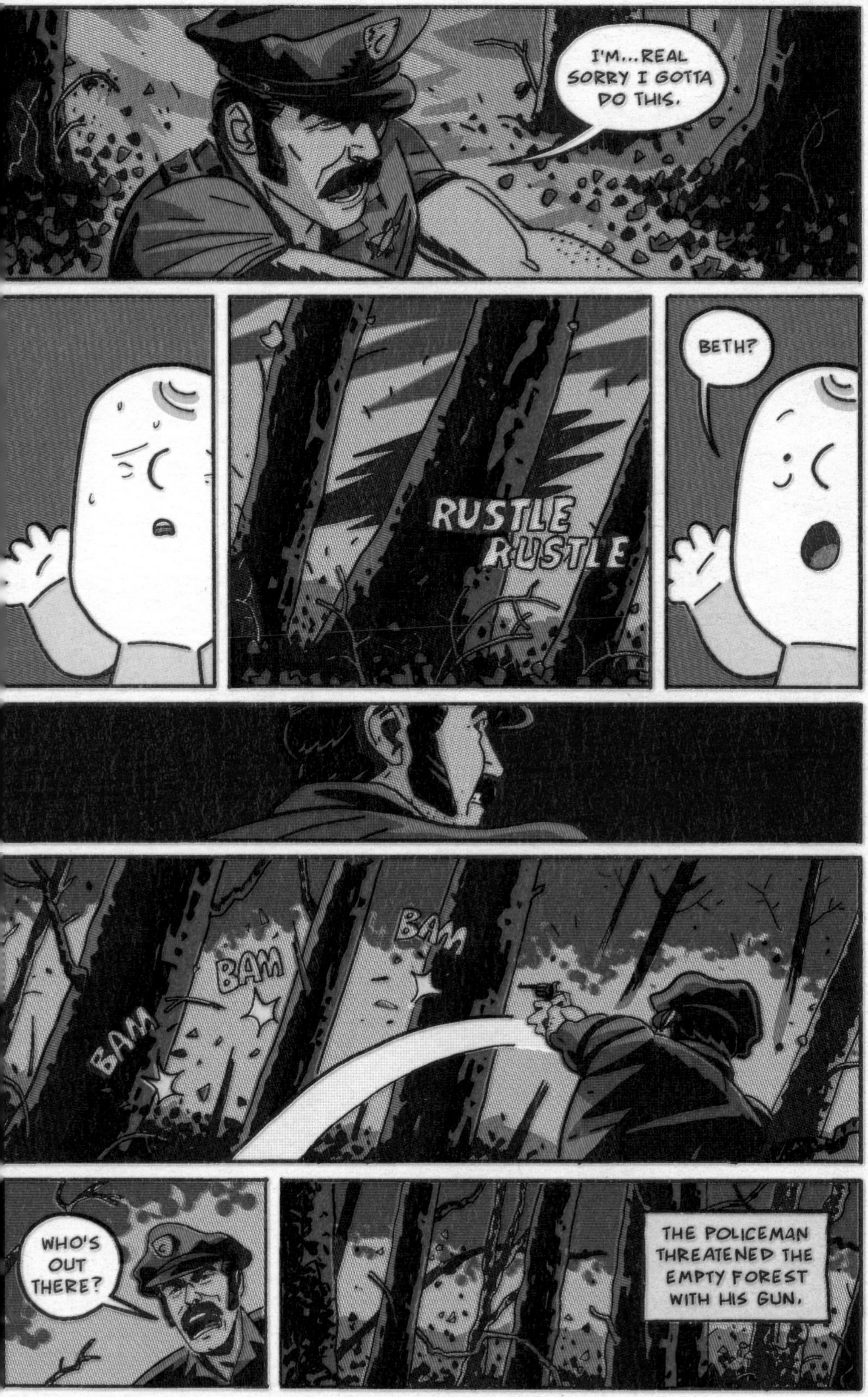
I'M...REAL SORRY I GOTTA DO THIS.
RUSTLE RUSTLE
BETH?
BAM
BAM
BAM
WHO'S OUT THERE?
THE POLICEMAN THREATENED THE EMPTY FOREST WITH HIS GUN.

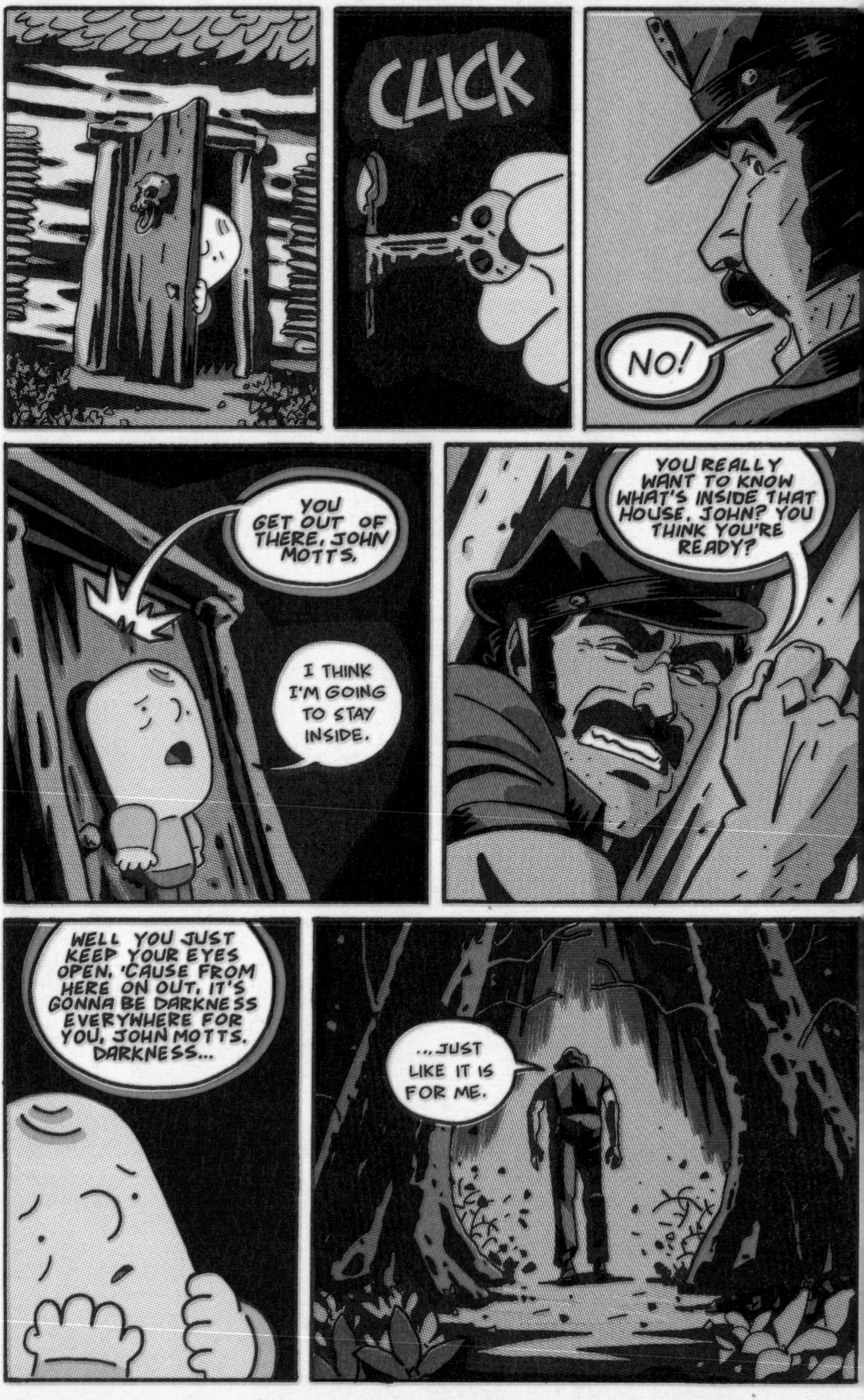
CLICK
NO!
YOU GET OUT OF THERE, JOHN MOTTS.
I THINK I'M GOING TO STAY INSIDE.
YOU REALLY WANT TO KNOW WHAT'S INSIDE THAT HOUSE, JOHN? YOU THINK YOU'RE READY?
WELL YOU JUST KEEP YOUR EYES OPEN, 'CAUSE FROM HERE ON OUT, IT'S GONNA BE DARKNESS EVERYWHERE FOR YOU, JOHN MOTTS. DARKNESS...
...JUST LIKE IT IS FOR ME.

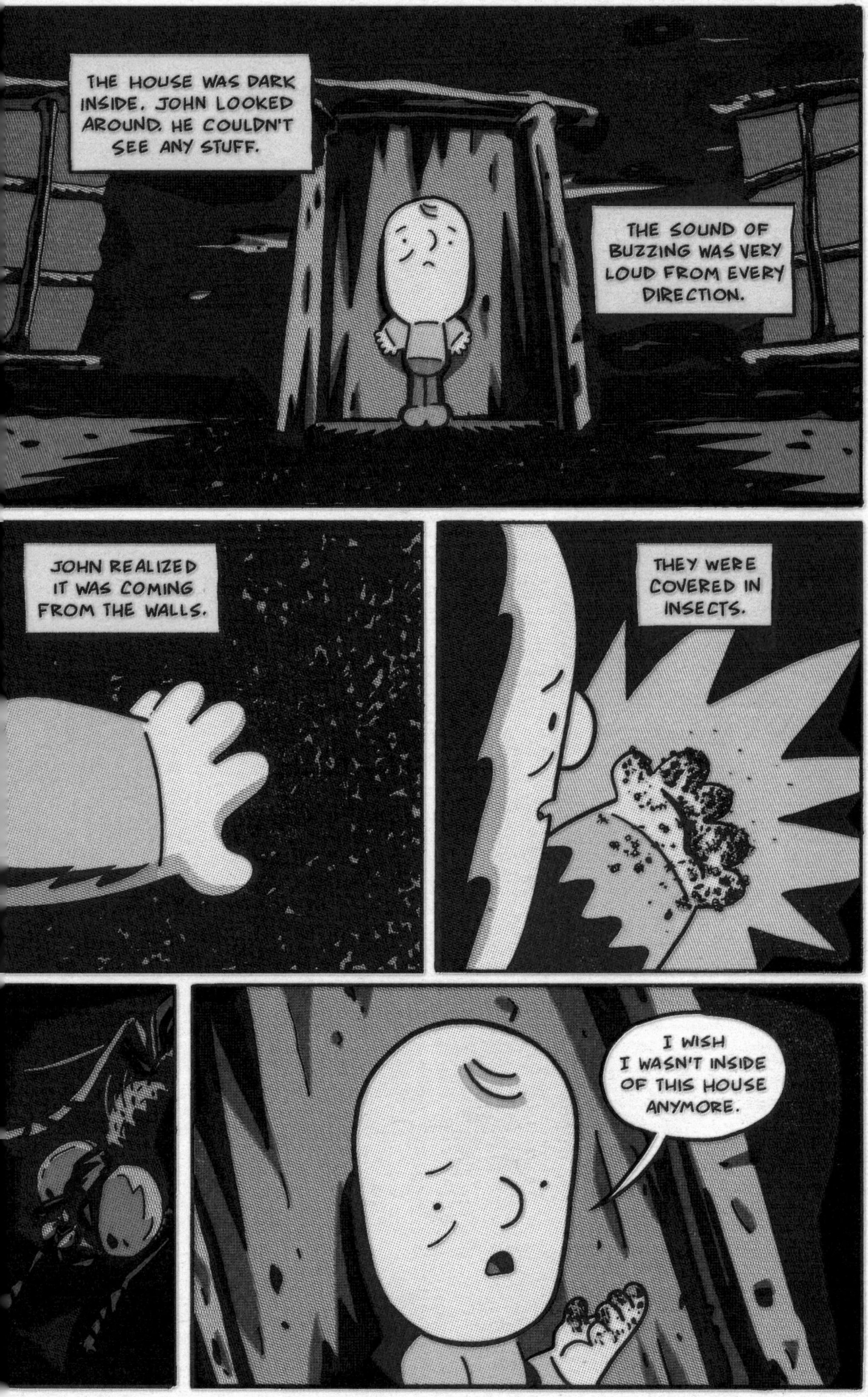
THE HOUSE WAS DARK INSIDE. JOHN LOOKED AROUND. HE COULDN'T SEE ANY STUFF.
THE SOUND OF BUZZING WAS VERY LOUD FROM EVERY DIRECTION.
JOHN REALIZED IT WAS COMING FROM THE WALLS.
THEY WERE COVERED IN INSECTS.
I WISH I WASN'T INSIDE OF THIS HOUSE ANYMORE.

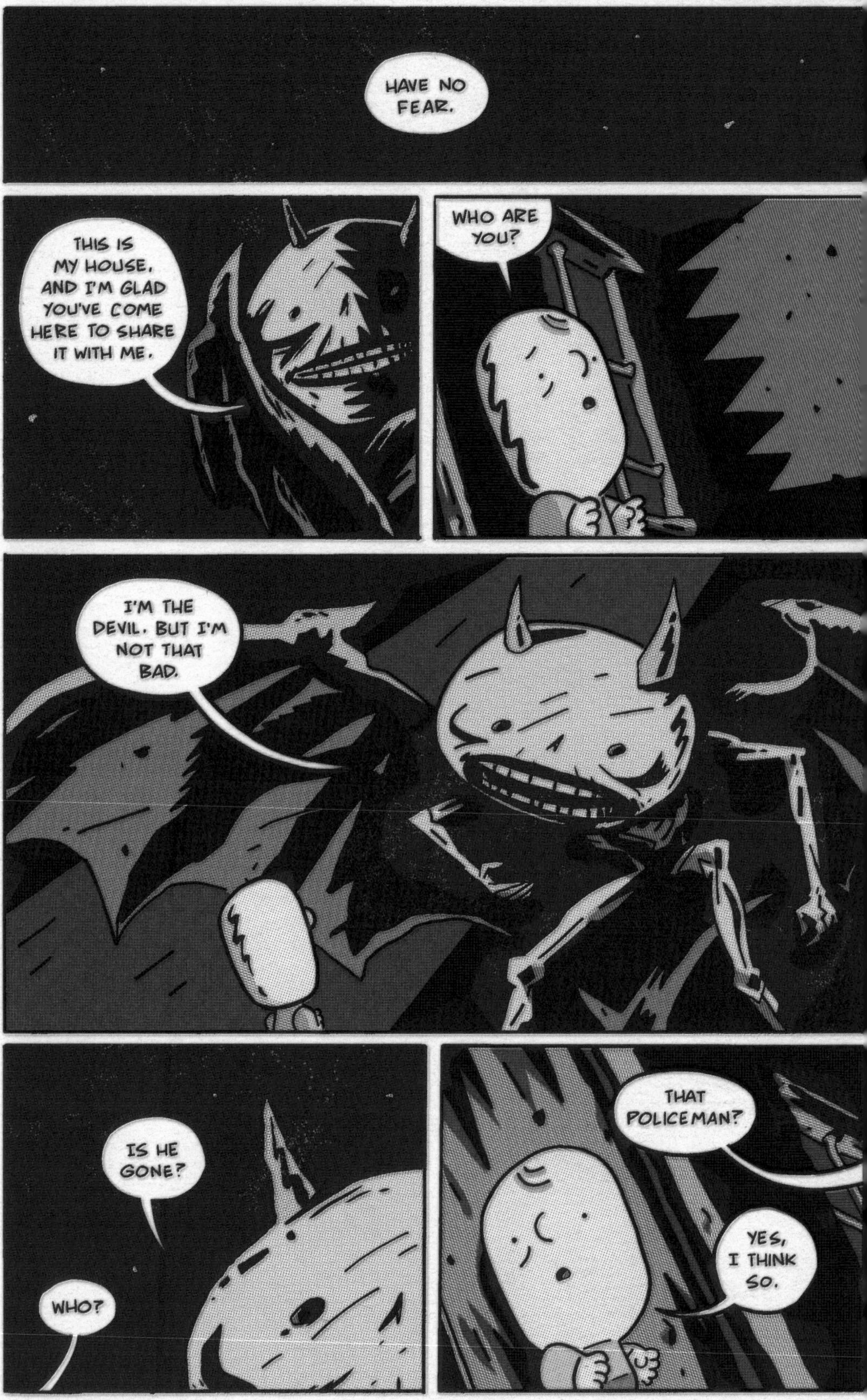
HAVE NO FEAR.
THIS IS MY HOUSE, AND I'M GLAD YOU'VE COME HERE TO SHARE IT WITH ME.
WHO ARE YOU?
I'M THE DEVIL. BUT I'M NOT THAT BAD.
IS HE GONE?
WHO?
THAT POLICEMAN?
YES, I THINK SO.

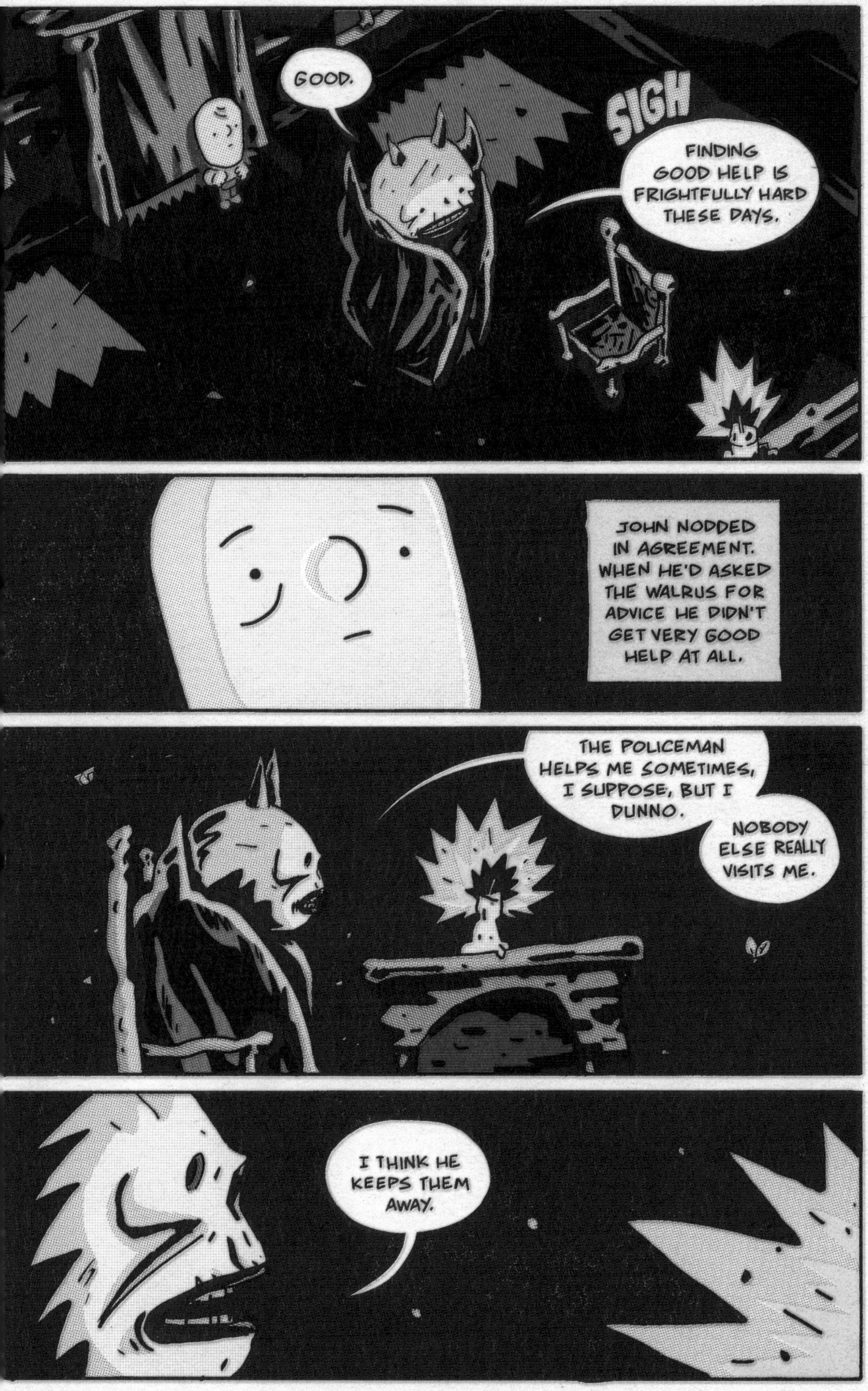
GOOD.
SIGH
FINDING GOOD HELP IS FRIGHTFULLY HARD THESE DAYS.
JOHN NODDED IN AGREEMENT. WHEN HE'D ASKED THE WALRUS FOR ADVICE HE DIDN'T GET VERY GOOD HELP AT ALL.
THE POLICEMAN HELPS ME SOMETIMES, I SUPPOSE, BUT I DUNNO.
NOBODY ELSE REALLY VISITS ME.
I THINK HE KEEPS THEM AWAY.

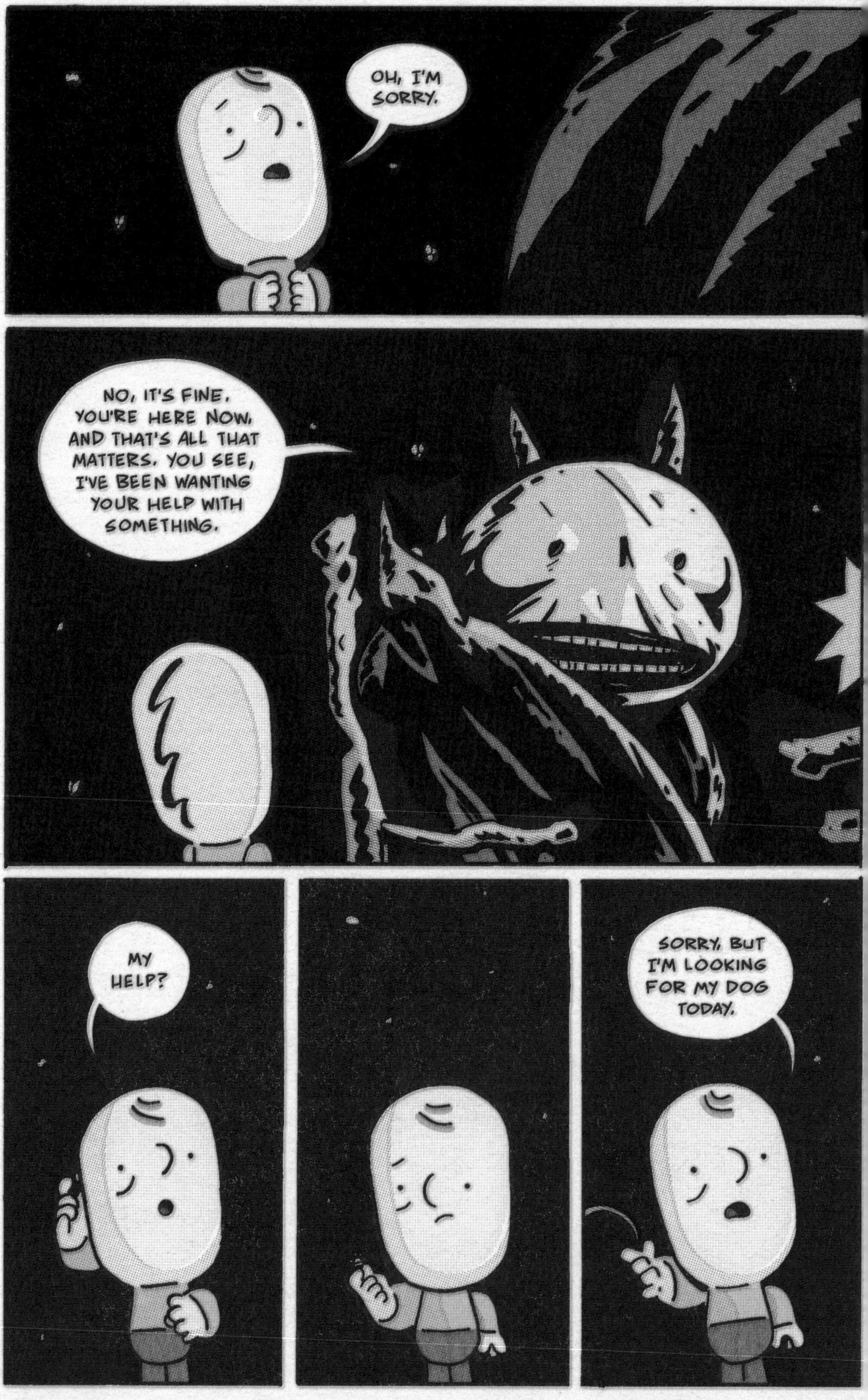
OH, I'M SORRY.
NO, IT'S FINE. YOU'RE HERE NOW, AND THAT'S ALL THAT MATTERS. YOU SEE, I'VE BEEN WANTING YOUR HELP WITH SOMETHING.
MY HELP?
SORRY, BUT I'M LOOKING FOR MY DOG TODAY.

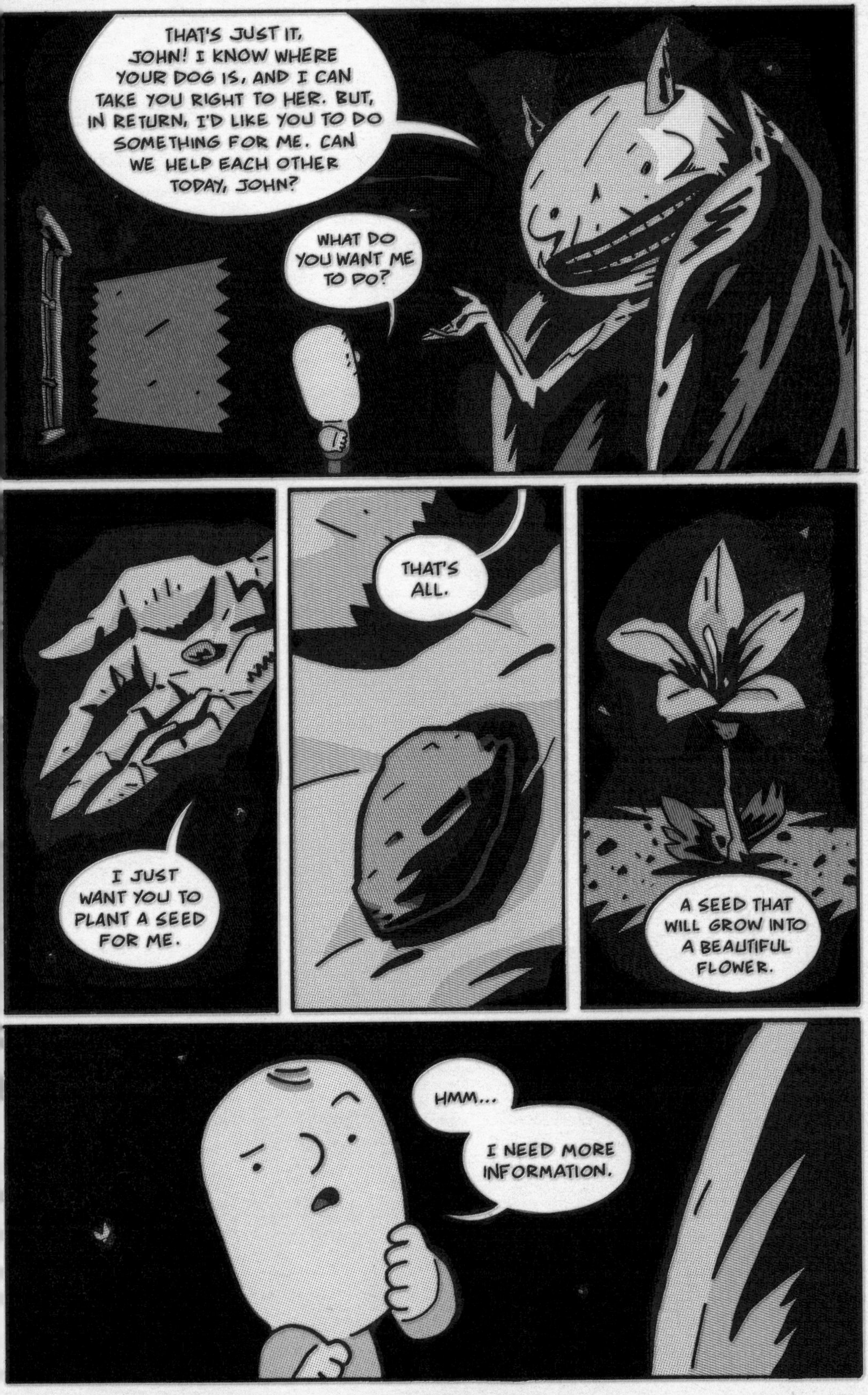
THAT'S JUST IT, JOHN! I KNOW WHERE YOUR DOG IS, AND I CAN TAKE YOU RIGHT TO HER. BUT, IN RETURN, I'D LIKE YOU TO DO SOMETHING FOR ME. CAN WE HELP EACH OTHER TODAY, JOHN?
WHAT DO YOU WANT ME TO DO?
I JUST WANT YOU TO PLANT A SEED FOR ME.
THAT'S ALL.
A SEED THAT WILL GROW INTO A BEAUTIFUL FLOWER.
HMM...
I NEED MORE INFORMATION.

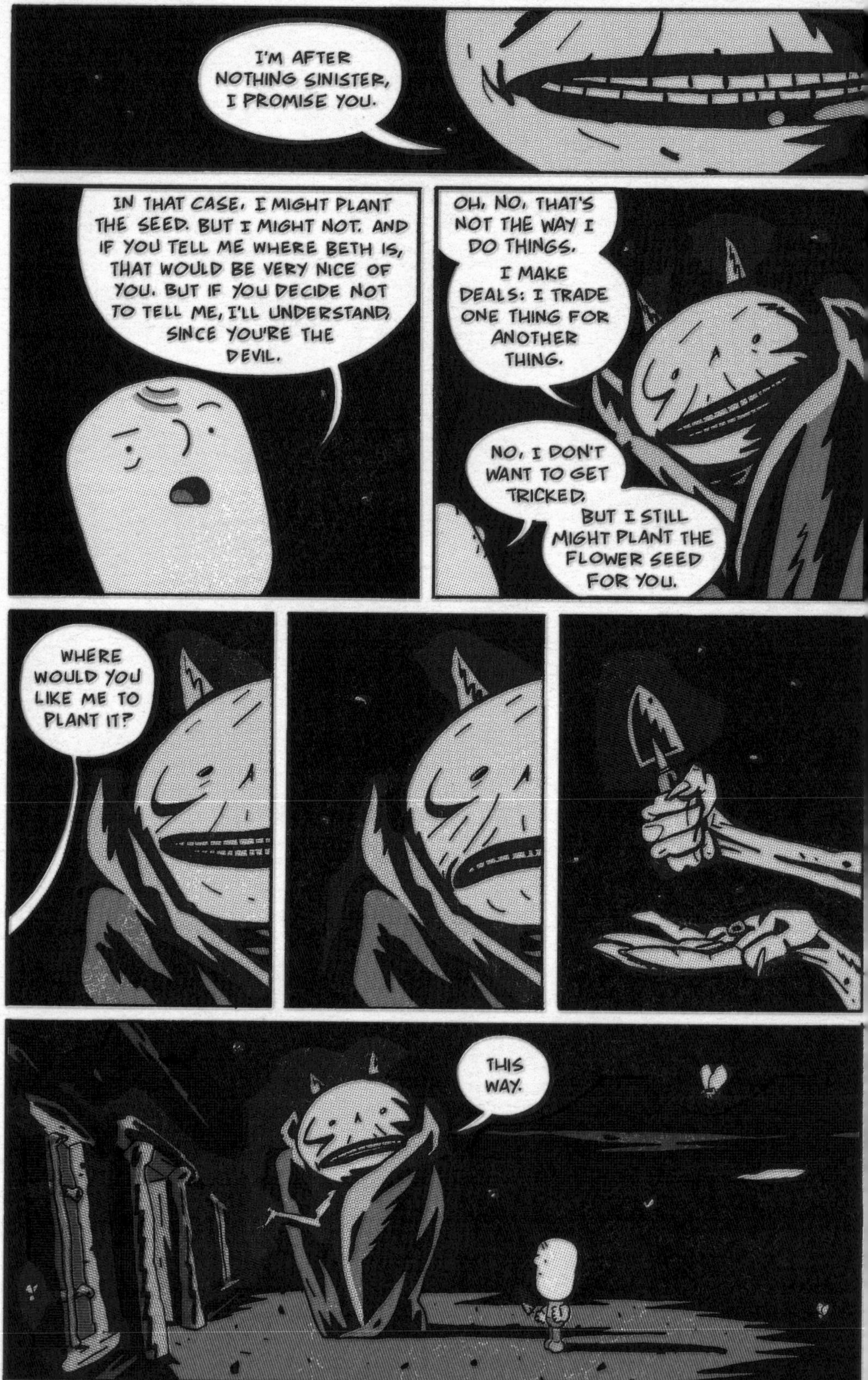
I'M AFTER NOTHING SINISTER, I PROMISE YOU.
IN THAT CASE, I MIGHT PLANT THE SEED. BUT I MIGHT NOT. AND IF YOU TELL ME WHERE BETH IS, THAT WOULD BE VERY NICE OF YOU. BUT IF YOU DECIDE NOT TO TELL ME, I'LL UNDERSTAND, SINCE YOU'RE THE DEVIL.
OH, NO, THAT'S NOT THE WAY I DO THINGS.
I MAKE DEALS: I TRADE ONE THING FOR ANOTHER THING.
NO, I DON'T WANT TO GET TRICKED.
BUT I STILL MIGHT PLANT THE FLOWER SEED FOR YOU.
WHERE WOULD YOU LIKE ME TO PLANT IT?
THIS WAY.

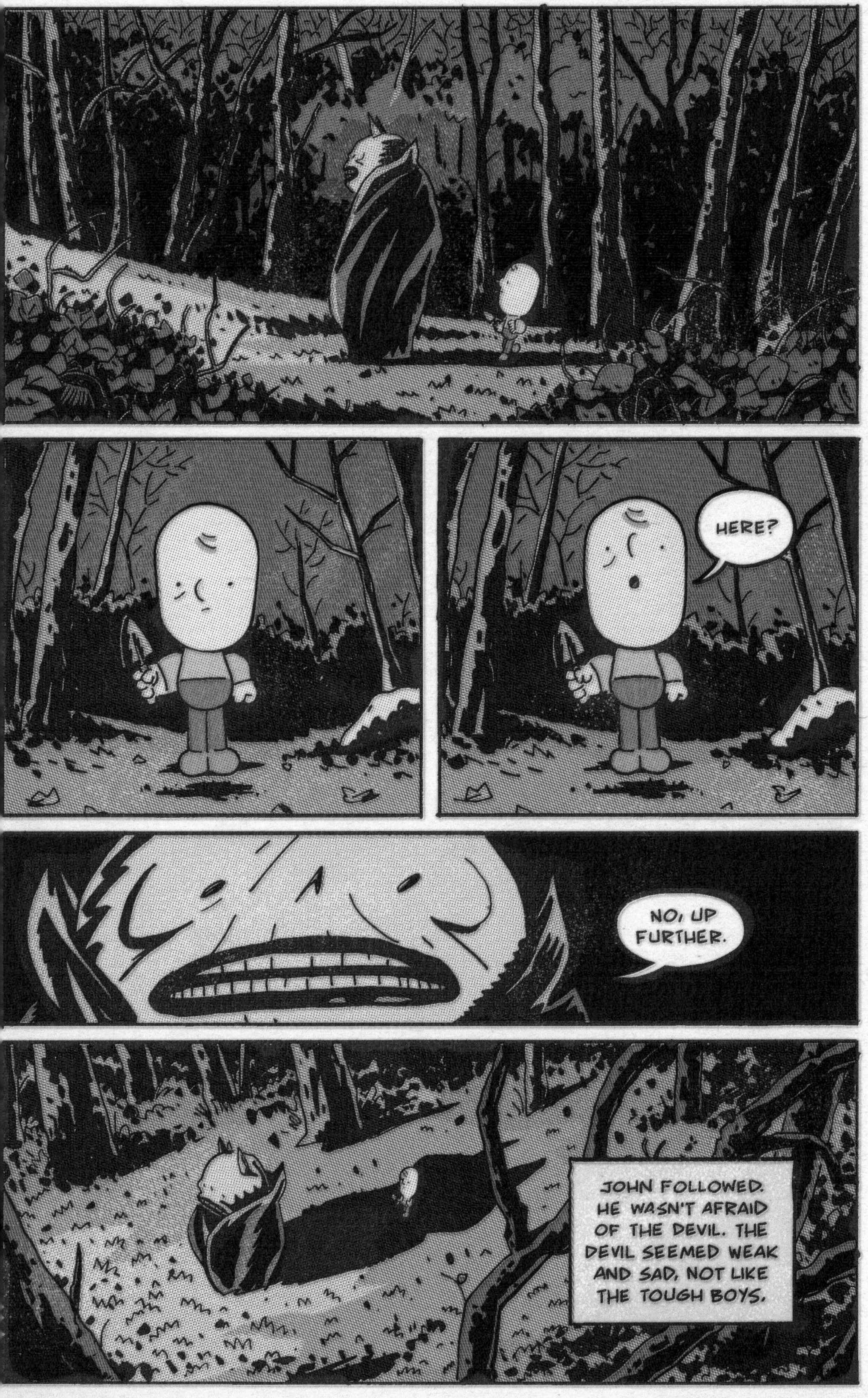
HERE?
NO, UP FURTHER.
JOHN FOLLOWED. HE WASN'T AFRAID OF THE DEVIL. THE DEVIL SEEMED WEAK AND SAD, NOT LIKE THE TOUGH BOYS.

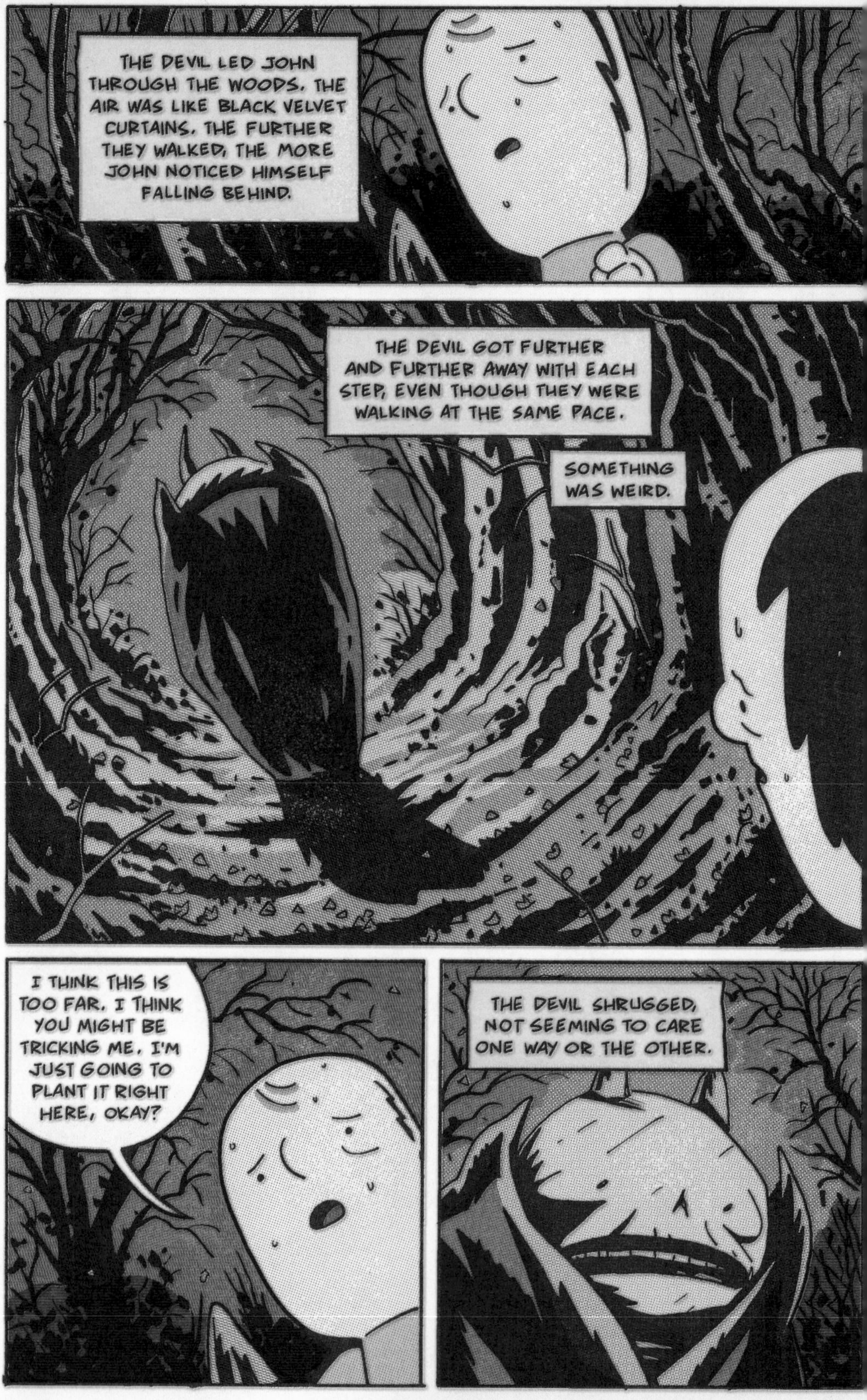
THE DEVIL LED JOHN THROUGH THE WOODS. THE AIR WAS LIKE BLACK VELVET CURTAINS. THE FURTHER THEY WALKED, THE MORE JOHN NOTICED HIMSELF FALLING BEHIND.
THE DEVIL GOT FURTHER AND FURTHER AWAY WITH EACH STEP, EVEN THOUGH THEY WERE WALKING AT THE SAME PACE.
SOMETHING WAS WEIRD.
I THINK THIS IS TOO FAR. I THINK YOU MIGHT BE TRICKING ME. I'M JUST GOING TO PLANT IT RIGHT HERE, OKAY?
THE DEVIL SHRUGGED, NOT SEEMING TO CARE ONE WAY OR THE OTHER.

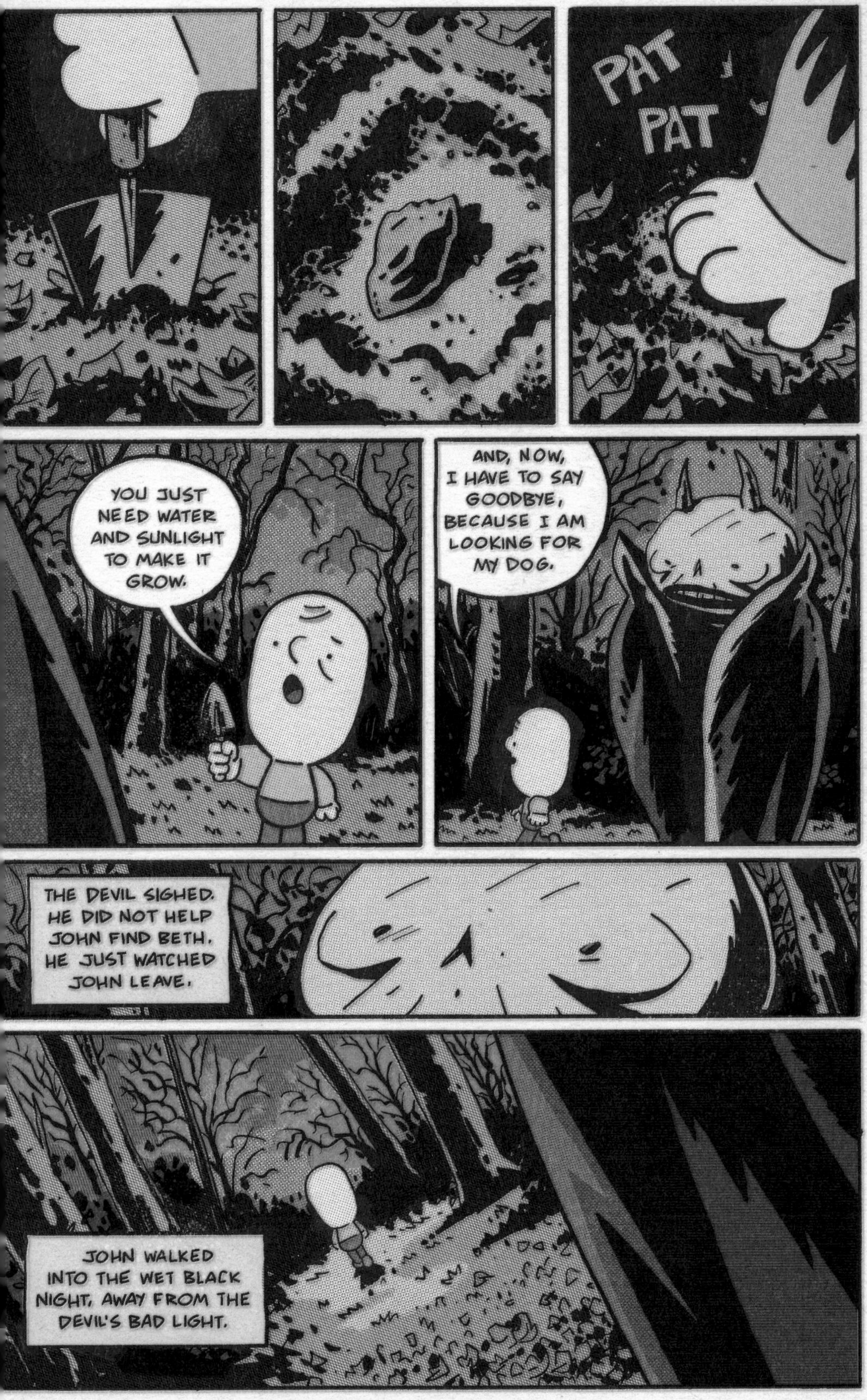
PAT
PAT
YOU JUST NEED WATER AND SUNLIGHT TO MAKE IT GROW.
AND, NOW, I HAVE TO SAY GOODBYE, BECAUSE I AM LOOKING FOR MY DOG.
THE DEVIL SIGHED. HE DID NOT HELP JOHN FIND BETH. HE JUST WATCHED JOHN LEAVE.
JOHN WALKED INTO THE WET BLACK NIGHT, AWAY FROM THE DEVIL'S BAD LIGHT.

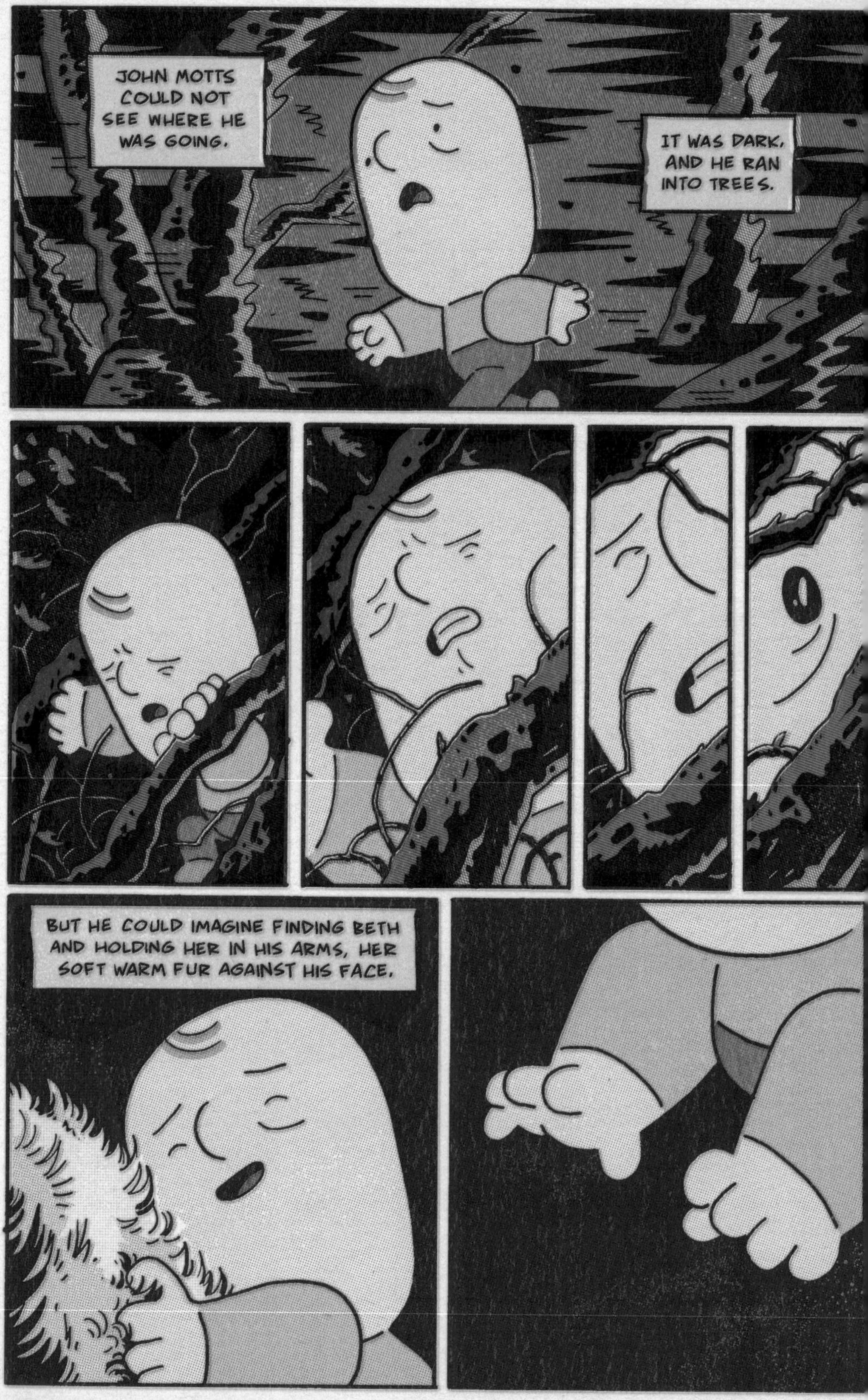
JOHN MOTTS COULD NOT SEE WHERE HE WAS GOING.
IT WAS DARK, AND HE RAN INTO TREES.
BUT HE COULD IMAGINE FINDING BETH AND HOLDING HER IN HIS ARMS, HER SOFT WARM FUR AGAINST HIS FACE.

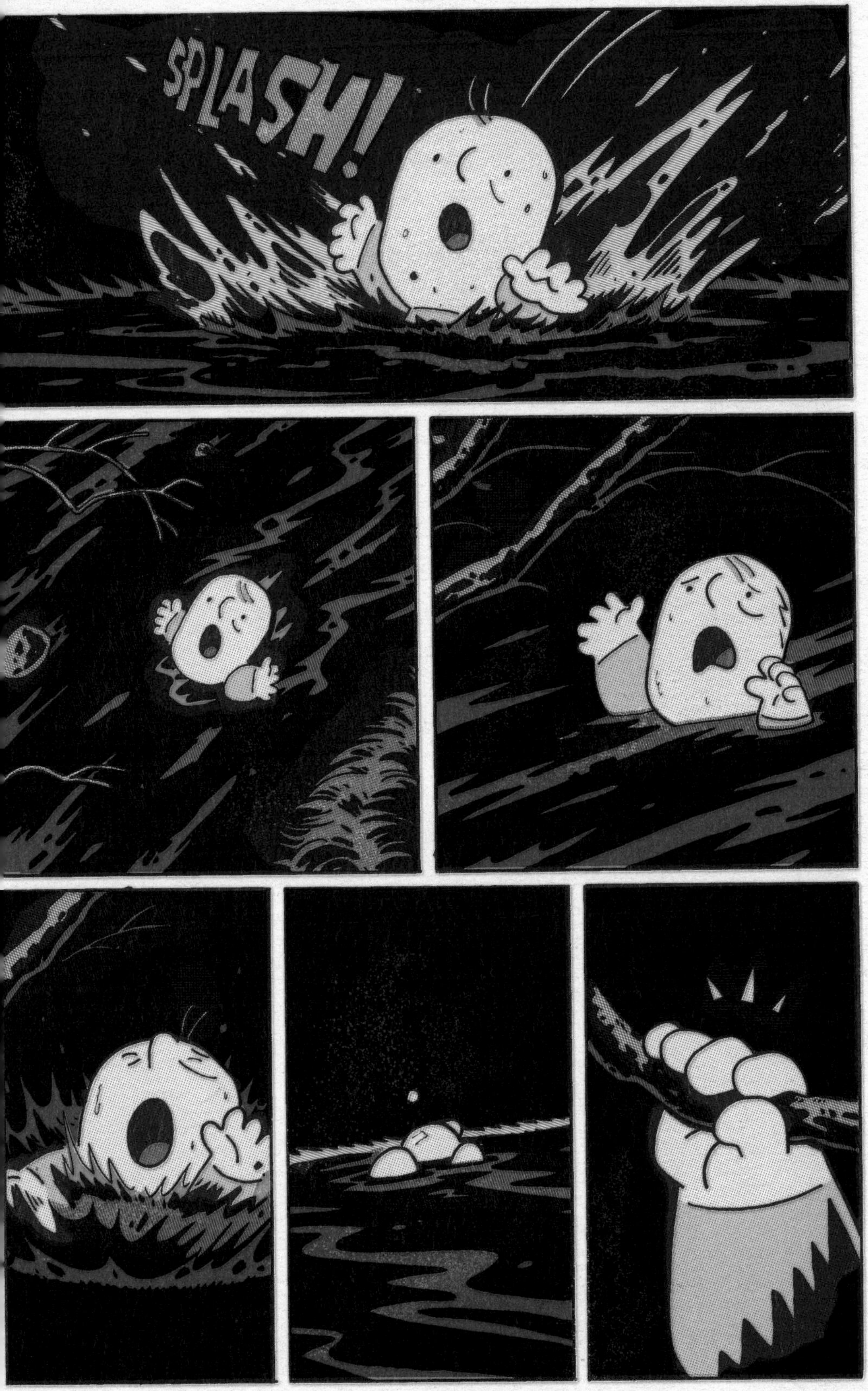
SPLASH!

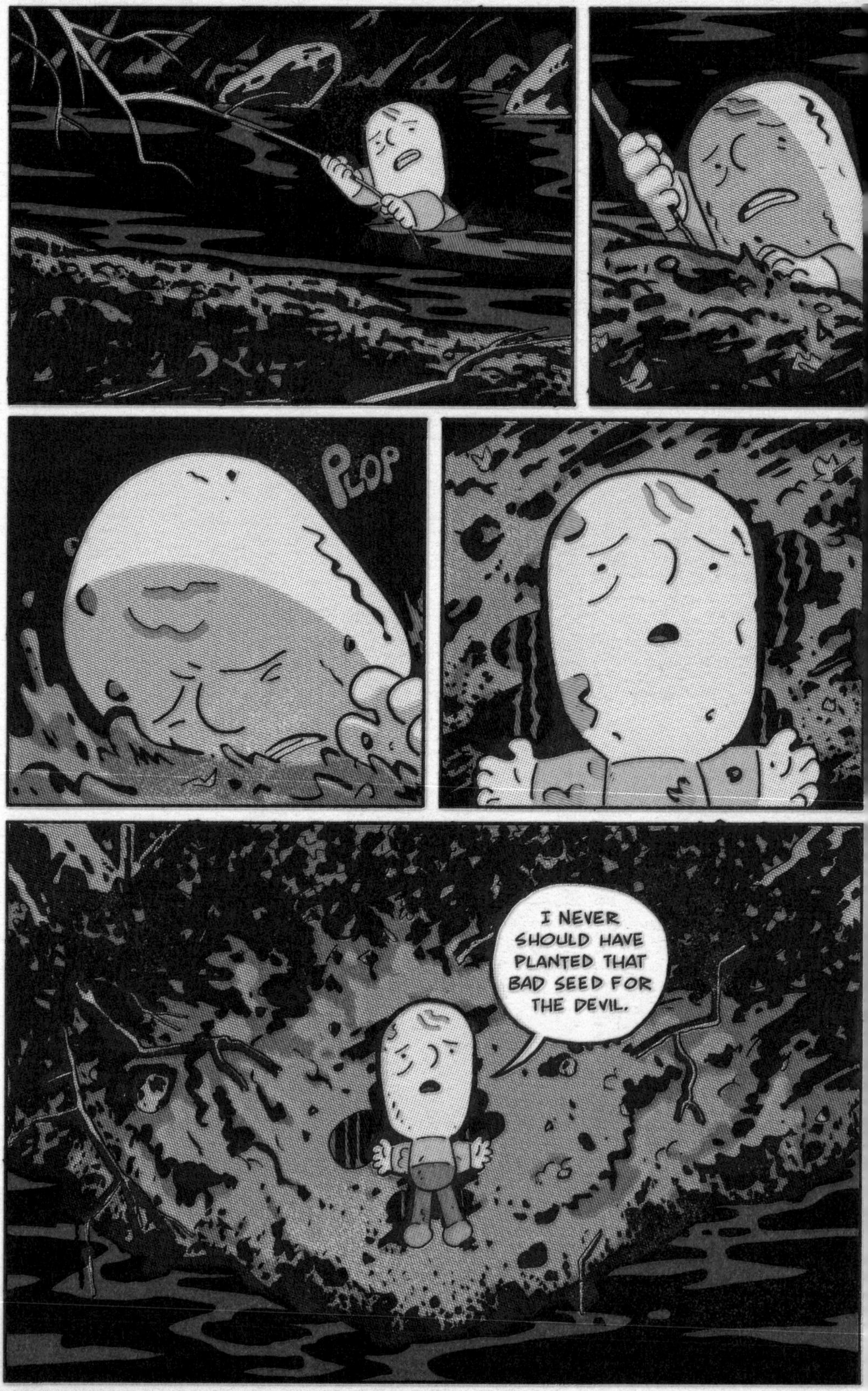
PLOP
I NEVER SHOULD HAVE PLANTED THAT BAD SEED FOR THE DEVIL.

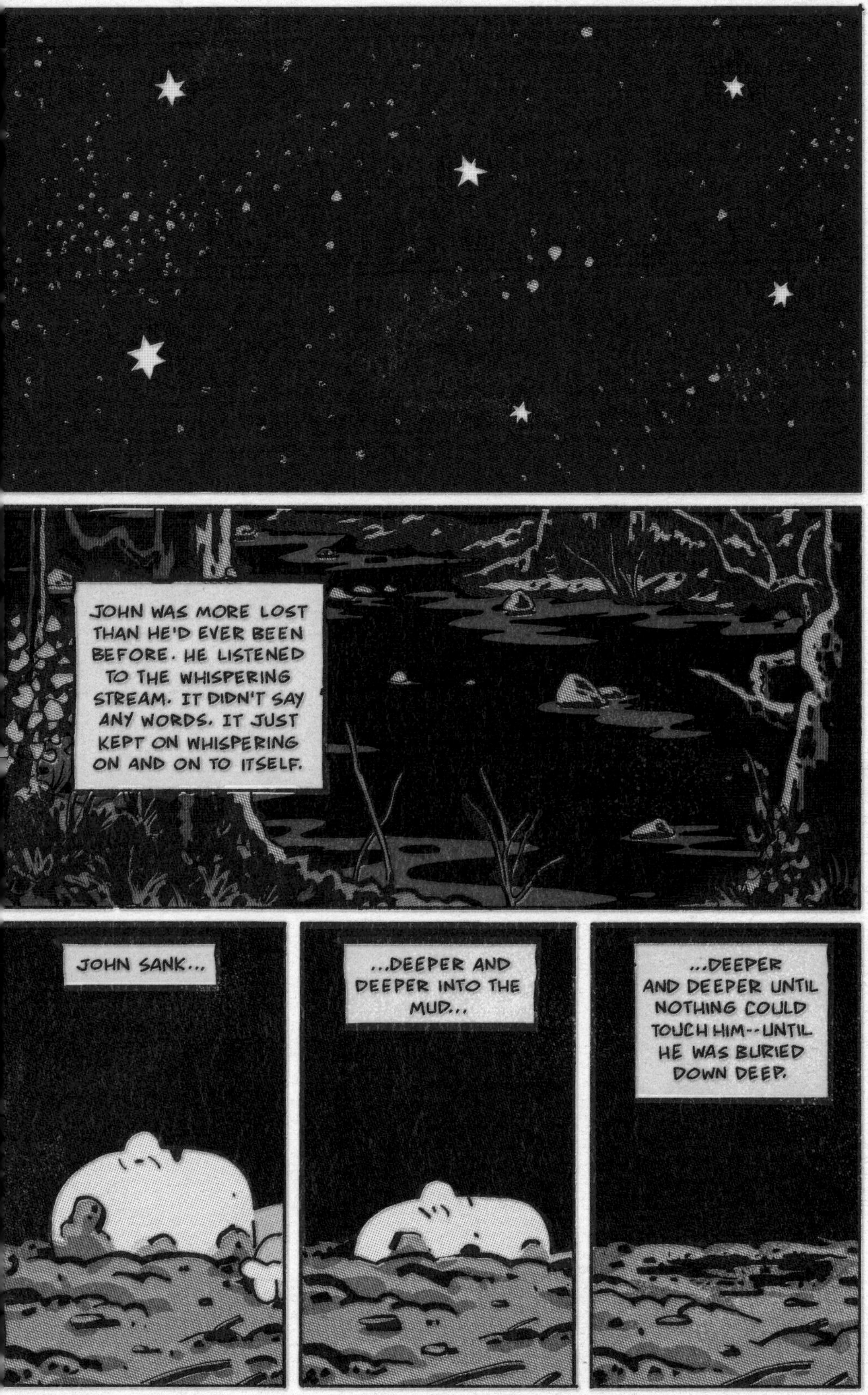
JOHN WAS MORE LOST THAN HE'D EVER BEEN BEFORE. HE LISTENED TO THE WHISPERING STREAM. IT DIDN'T SAY ANY WORDS. IT JUST KEPT ON WHISPERING ON AND ON TO ITSELF.
JOHN SANK...
...DEEPER AND DEEPER INTO THE MUD...
...DEEPER AND DEEPER UNTIL NOTHING COULD TOUCH HIM--UNTIL HE WAS BURIED DOWN DEEP.

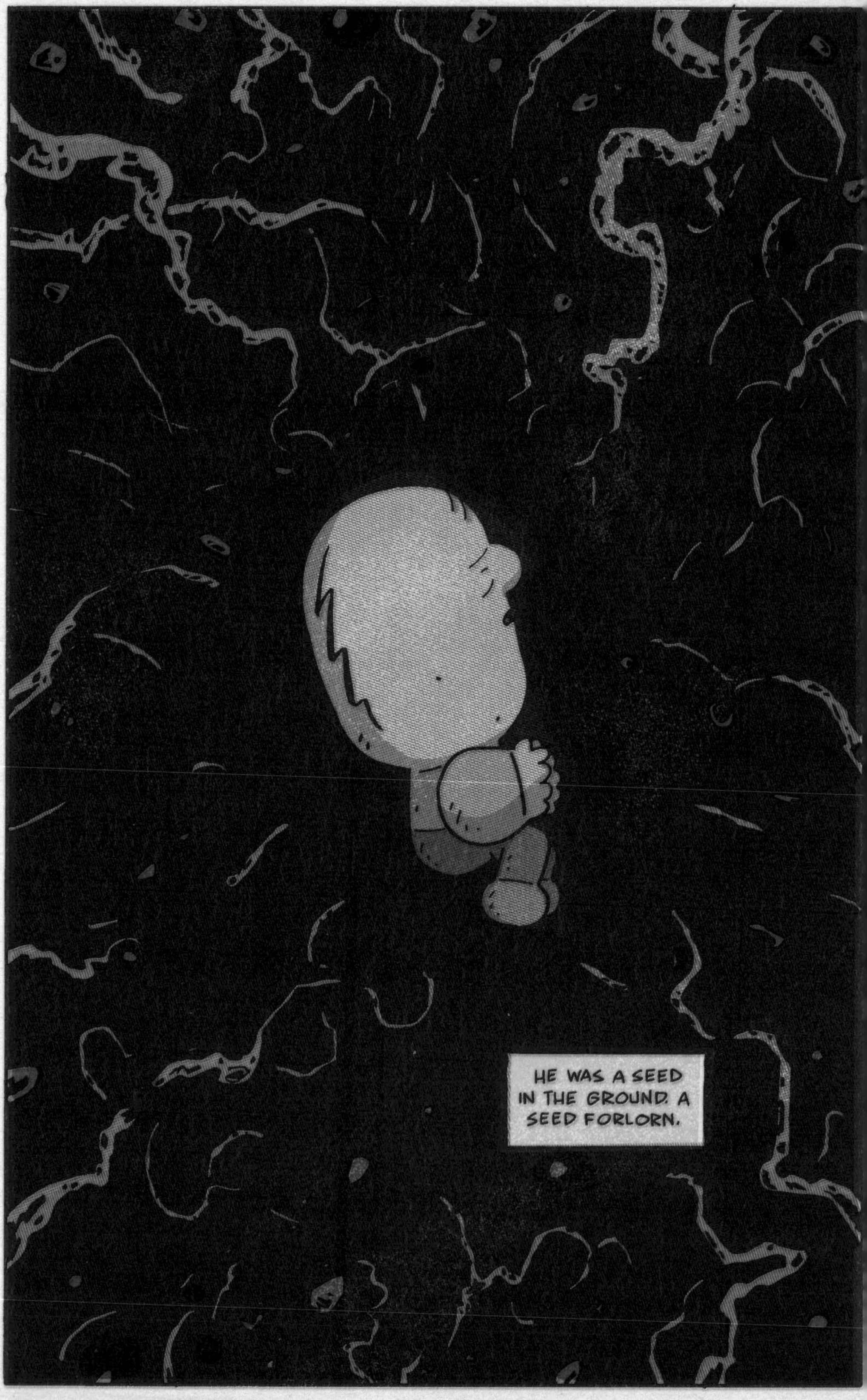
HE WAS A SEED IN THE GROUND. A SEED FORLORN.

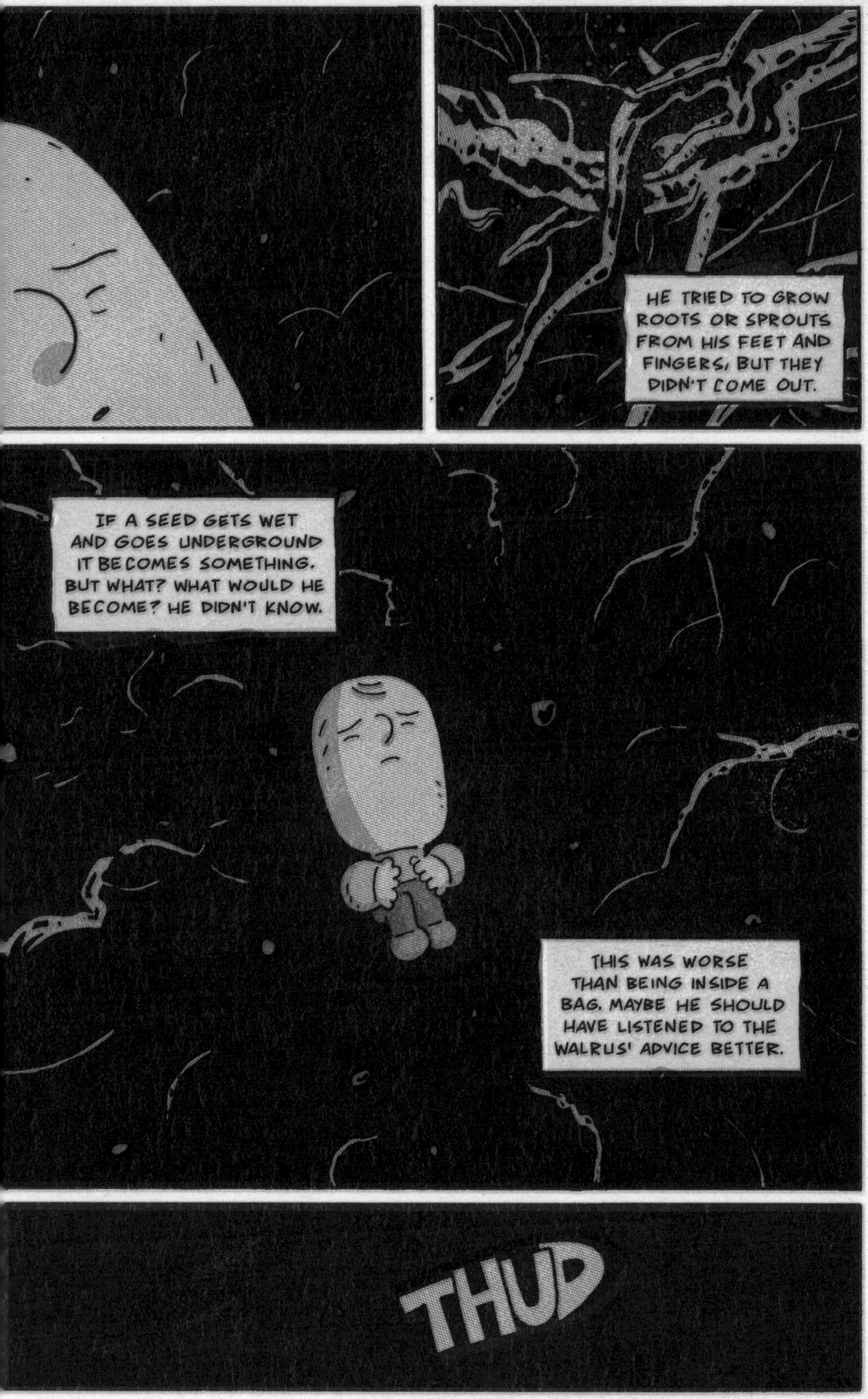
HE TRIED TO GROW ROOTS OR SPROUTS FROM HIS FEET AND FINGERS, BUT THEY DIDN'T COME OUT.
IF A SEED GETS WET AND GOES UNDERGROUND IT BECOMES SOMETHING. BUT WHAT? WHAT WOULD HE BECOME? HE DIDN'T KNOW.
THIS WAS WORSE THAN BEING INSIDE A BAG. MAYBE HE SHOULD HAVE LISTENED TO THE WALRUS' ADVICE BETTER.
THUD

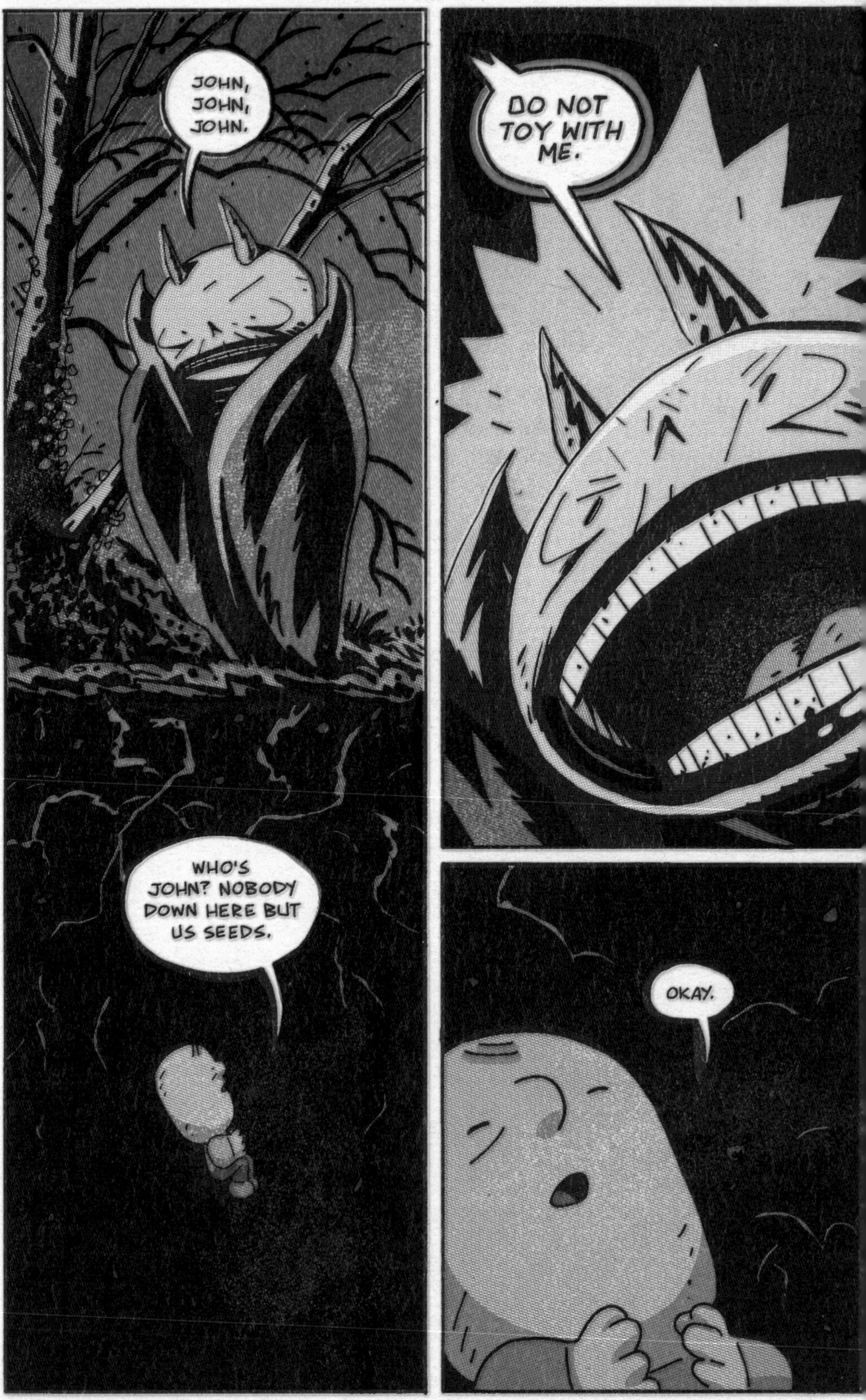
JOHN, JOHN, JOHN.
DO NOT TOY WITH ME.
WHO'S JOHN? NOBODY DOWN HERE BUT US SEEDS.
OKAY.

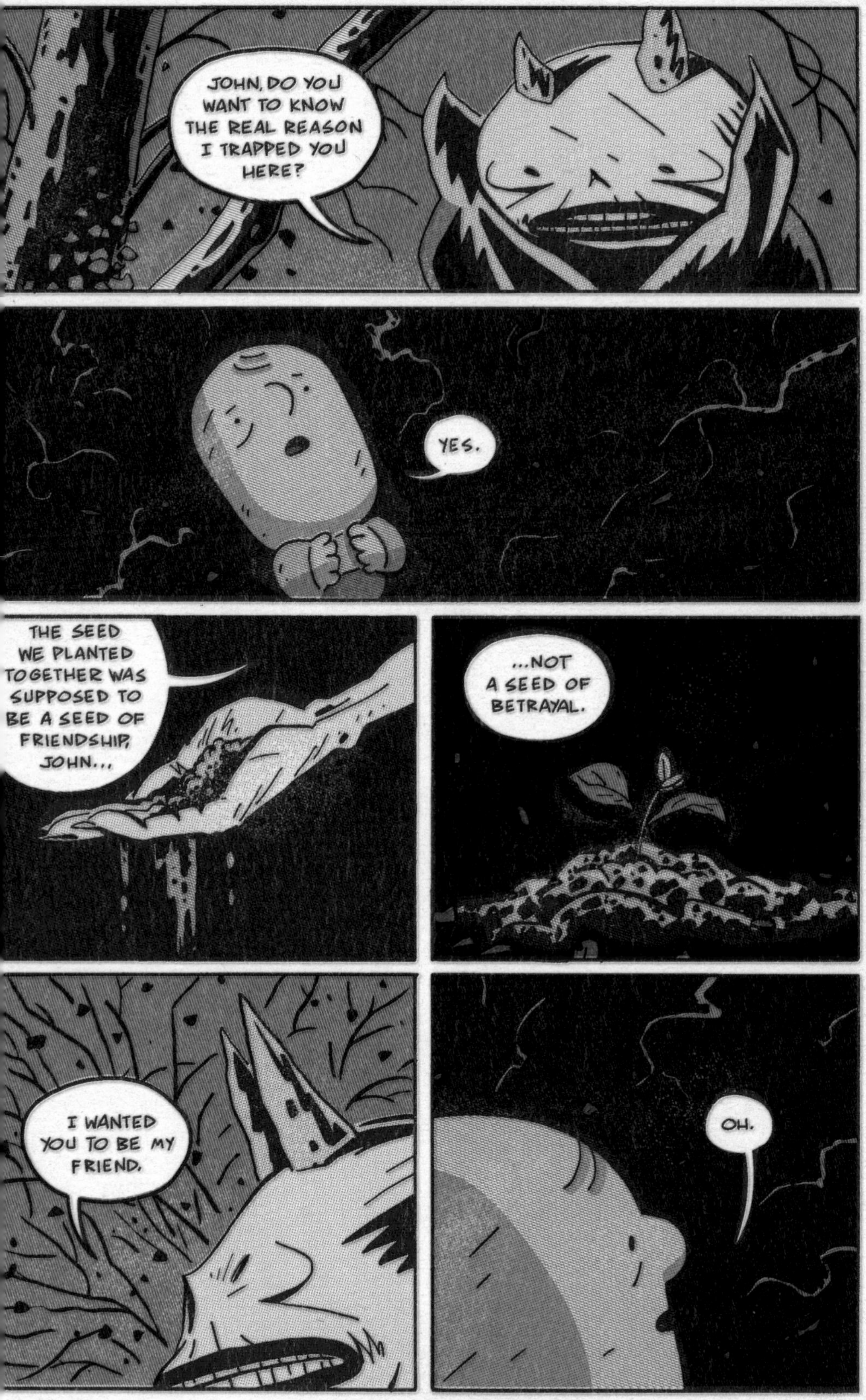
JOHN, DO YOU WANT TO KNOW THE REAL REASON I TRAPPED YOU HERE?
YES.
THE SEED WE PLANTED TOGETHER WAS SUPPOSED TO BE A SEED OF FRIENDSHIP, JOHN...
...NOT A SEED OF BETRAYAL.
I WANTED YOU TO BE MY FRIEND.
OH.

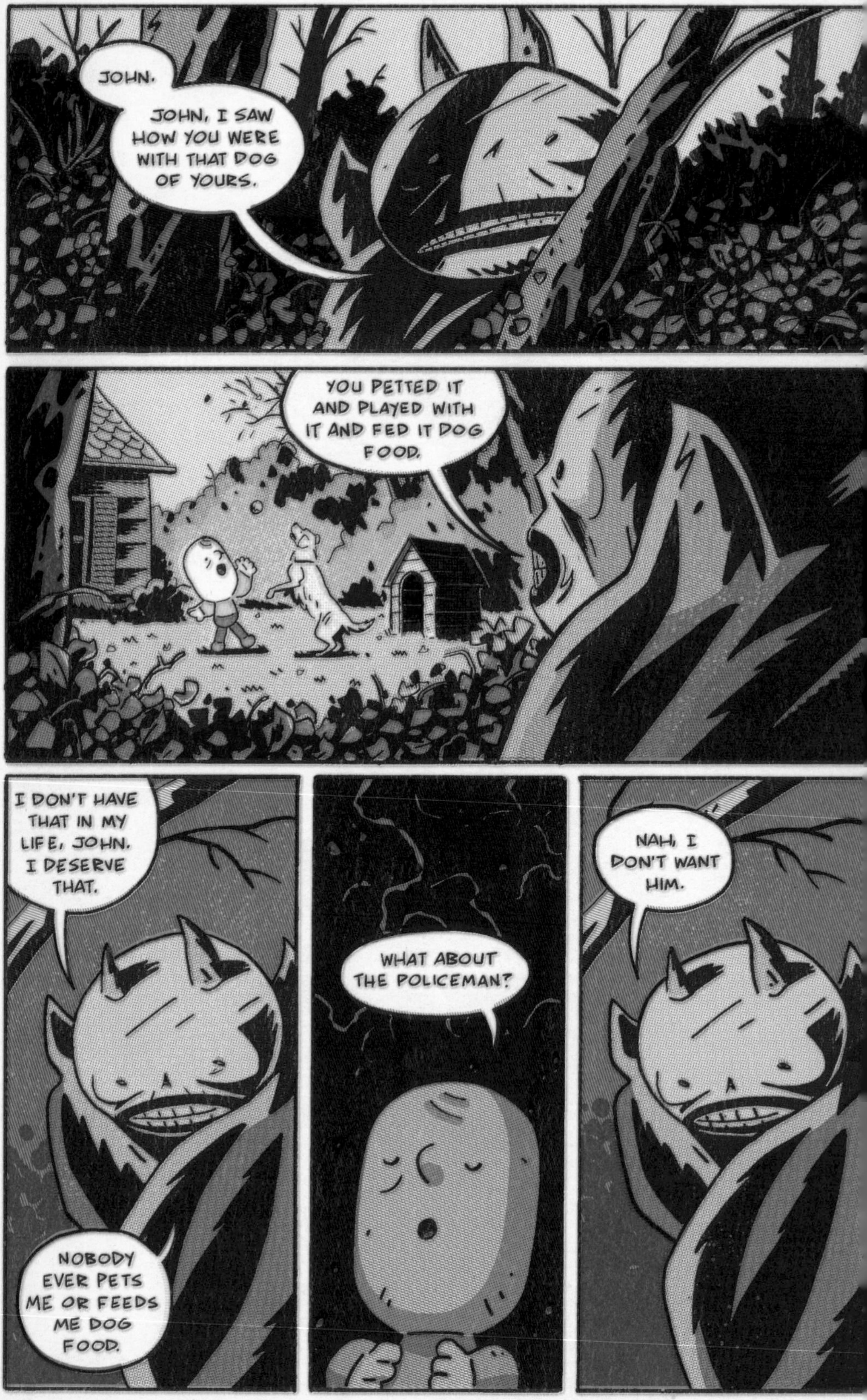
JOHN.
JOHN, I SAW HOW YOU WERE WITH THAT DOG OF YOURS.
YOU PETTED IT AND PLAYED WITH IT AND FED IT DOG FOOD.
I DON'T HAVE THAT IN MY LIFE, JOHN. I DESERVE THAT.
NOBODY EVER PETS ME OR FEEDS ME DOG FOOD.
WHAT ABOUT THE POLICEMAN?
NAH, I DON'T WANT HIM.

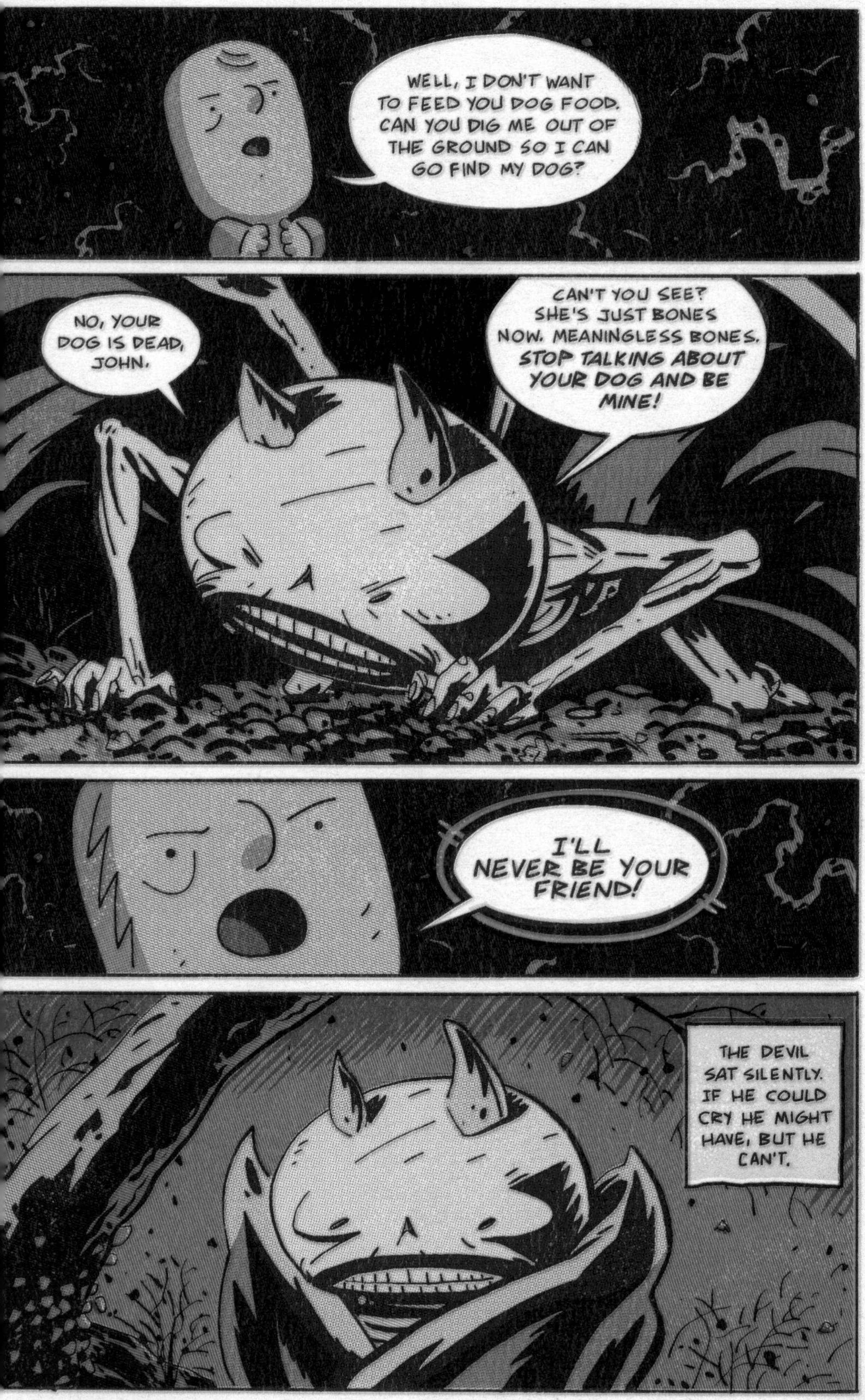
WELL, I DON'T WANT TO FEED YOU DOG FOOD. CAN YOU DIG ME OUT OF THE GROUND SO I CAN GO FIND MY DOG?
NO, YOUR DOG IS DEAD, JOHN.
CAN'T YOU SEE? SHE'S JUST BONES NOW. MEANINGLESS BONES. STOP TALKING ABOUT YOUR DOG AND BE MINE!
I'LL NEVER BE YOUR FRIEND!
THE DEVIL SAT SILENTLY. IF HE COULD CRY HE MIGHT HAVE, BUT HE CAN'T.

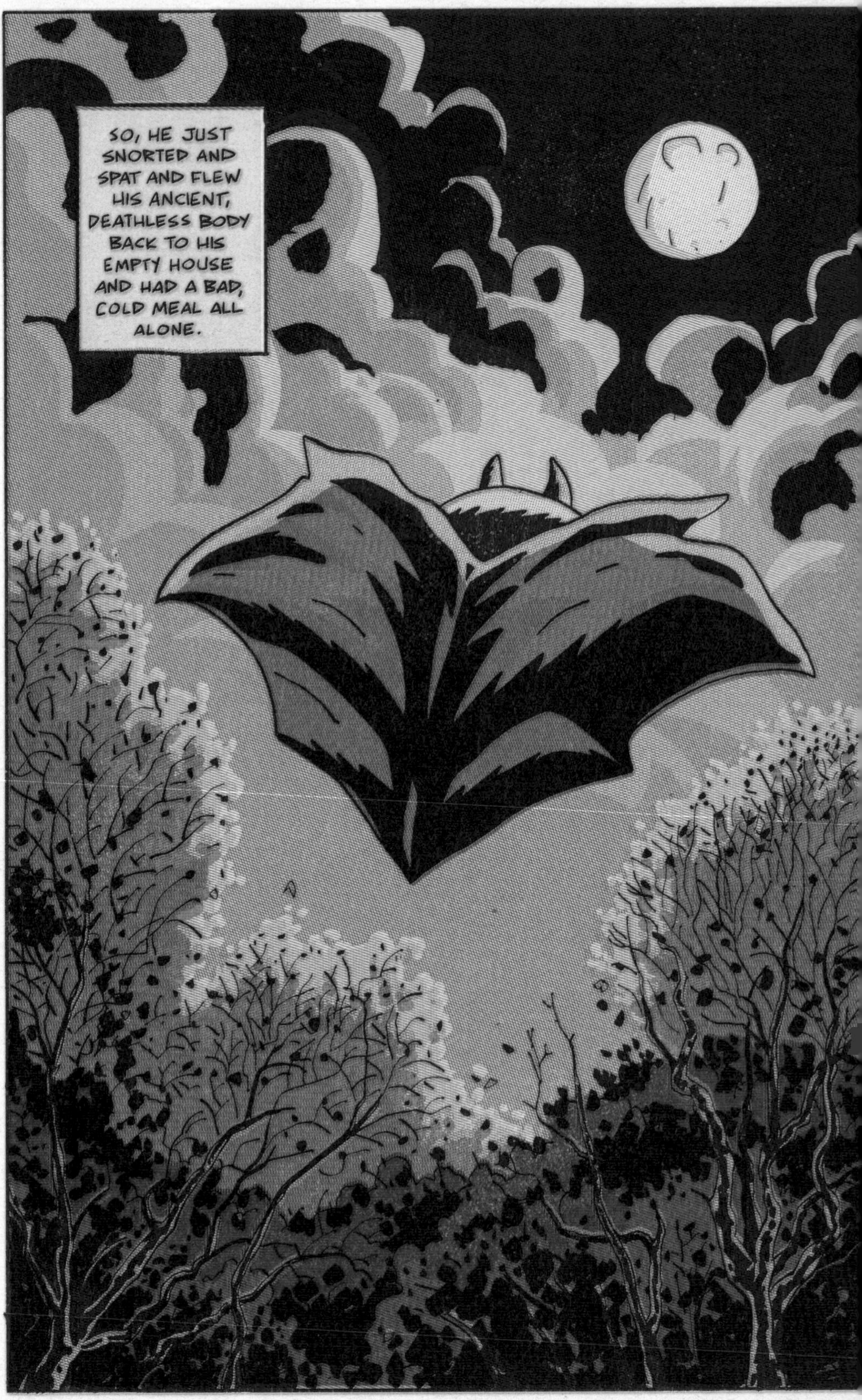
SO, HE JUST SNORTED AND SPAT AND FLEW HIS ANCIENT, DEATHLESS BODY BACK TO HIS EMPTY HOUSE AND HAD A BAD, COLD MEAL ALL ALONE.

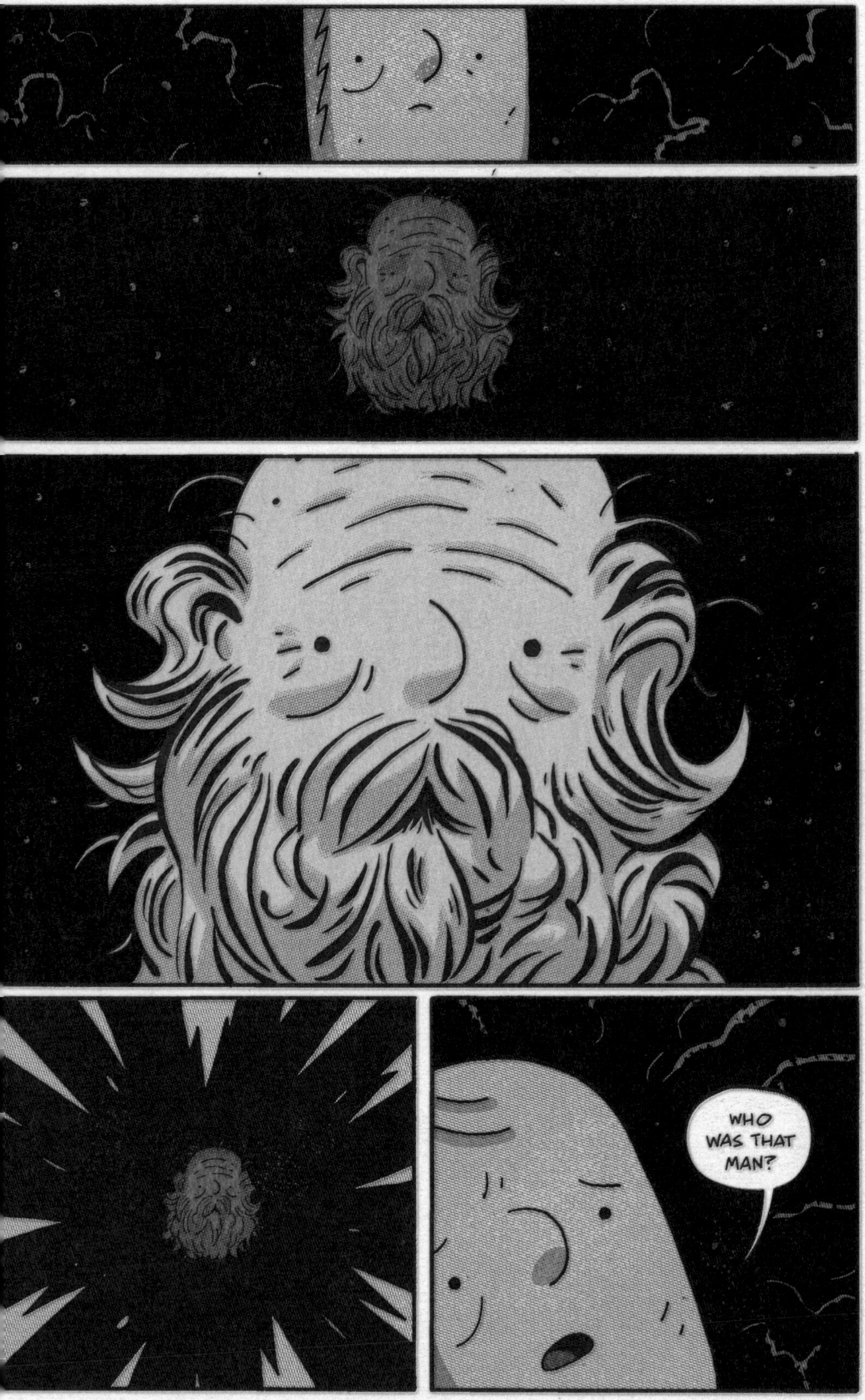
WHO WAS THAT MAN?

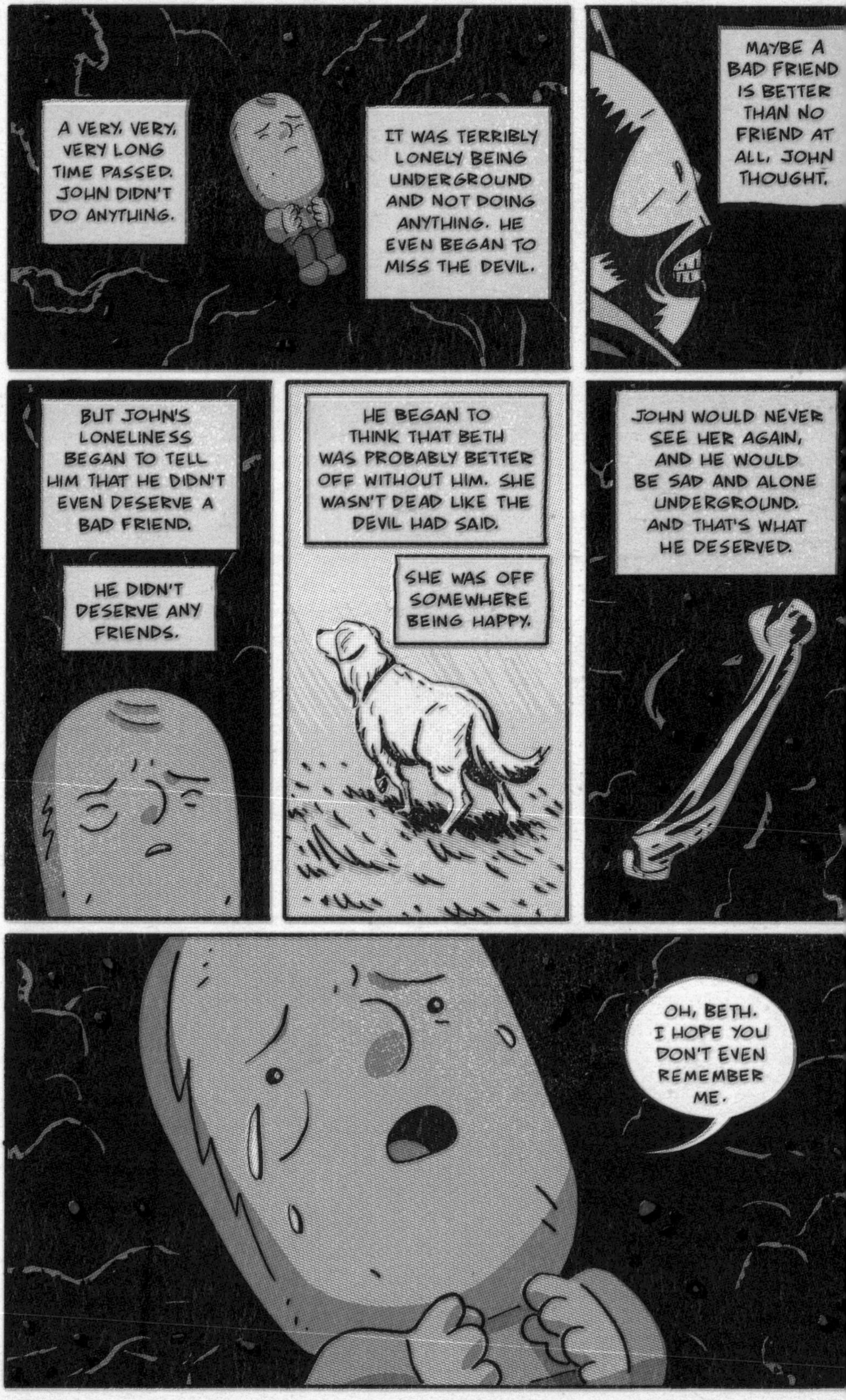
A VERY, VERY, VERY LONG TIME PASSED. JOHN DIDN'T DO ANYTHING.
IT WAS TERRIBLY LONELY BEING UNDERGROUND AND NOT DOING ANYTHING. HE EVEN BEGAN TO MISS THE DEVIL.
MAYBE A BAD FRIEND IS BETTER THAN NO FRIEND AT ALL, JOHN THOUGHT.
BUT JOHN'S LONELINESS BEGAN TO TELL HIM THAT HE DIDN'T EVEN DESERVE A BAD FRIEND.
HE DIDN'T DESERVE ANY FRIENDS.
HE BEGAN TO THINK THAT BETH WAS PROBABLY BETTER OFF WITHOUT HIM. SHE WASN'T DEAD LIKE THE DEVIL HAD SAID.
SHE WAS OFF SOMEWHERE BEING HAPPY.
JOHN WOULD NEVER SEE HER AGAIN, AND HE WOULD BE SAD AND ALONE UNDERGROUND. AND THAT'S WHAT HE DESERVED.
OH, BETH. I HOPE YOU DON'T EVEN REMEMBER ME.

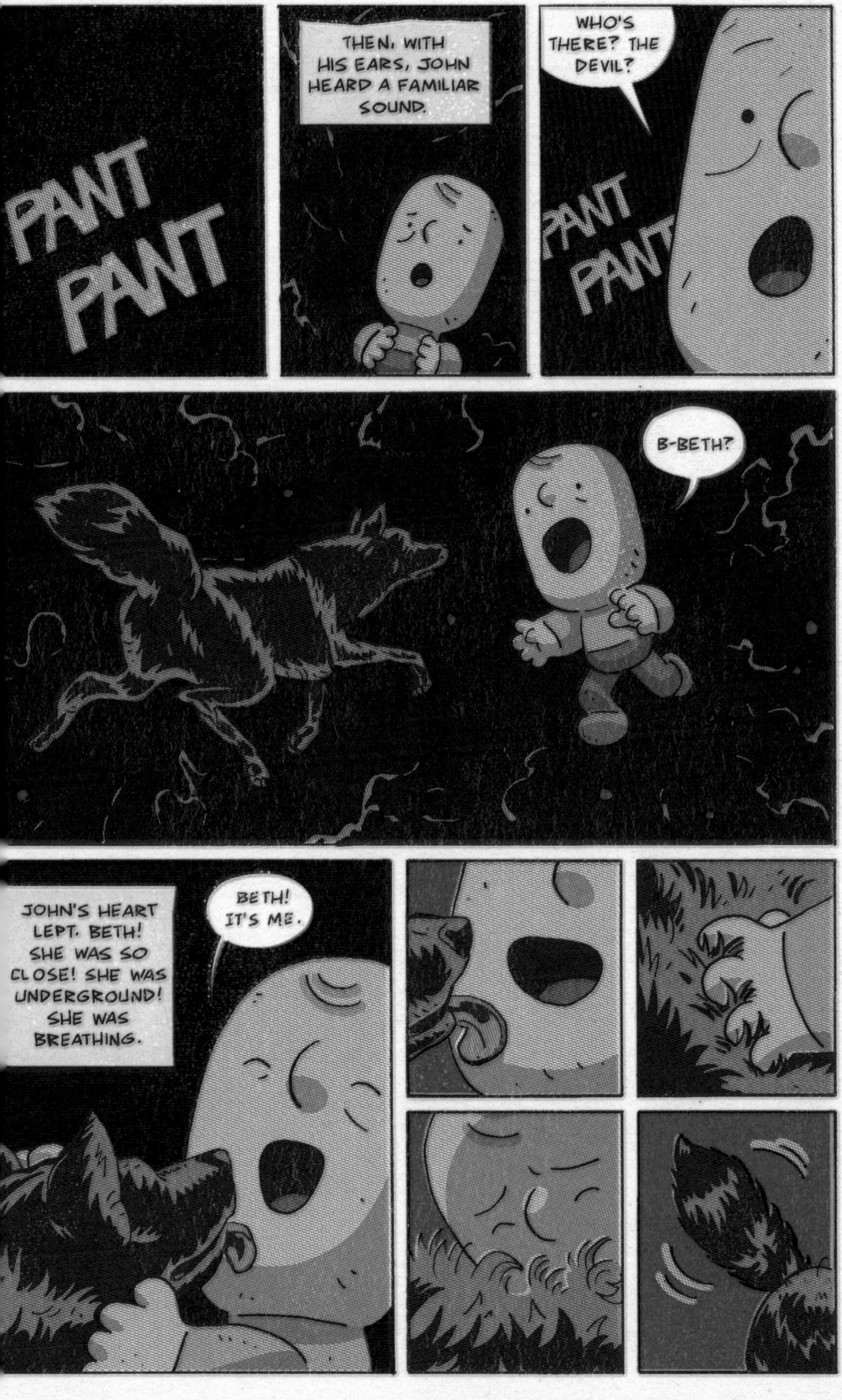
PANT PANT
THEN, WITH HIS EARS, JOHN HEARD A FAMILIAR SOUND.
WHO'S THERE? THE DEVIL?
PANT PANT
B-BETH?
JOHN'S HEART LEPT. BETH! SHE WAS SO CLOSE! SHE WAS UNDERGROUND! SHE WAS BREATHING.
BETH! IT'S ME.

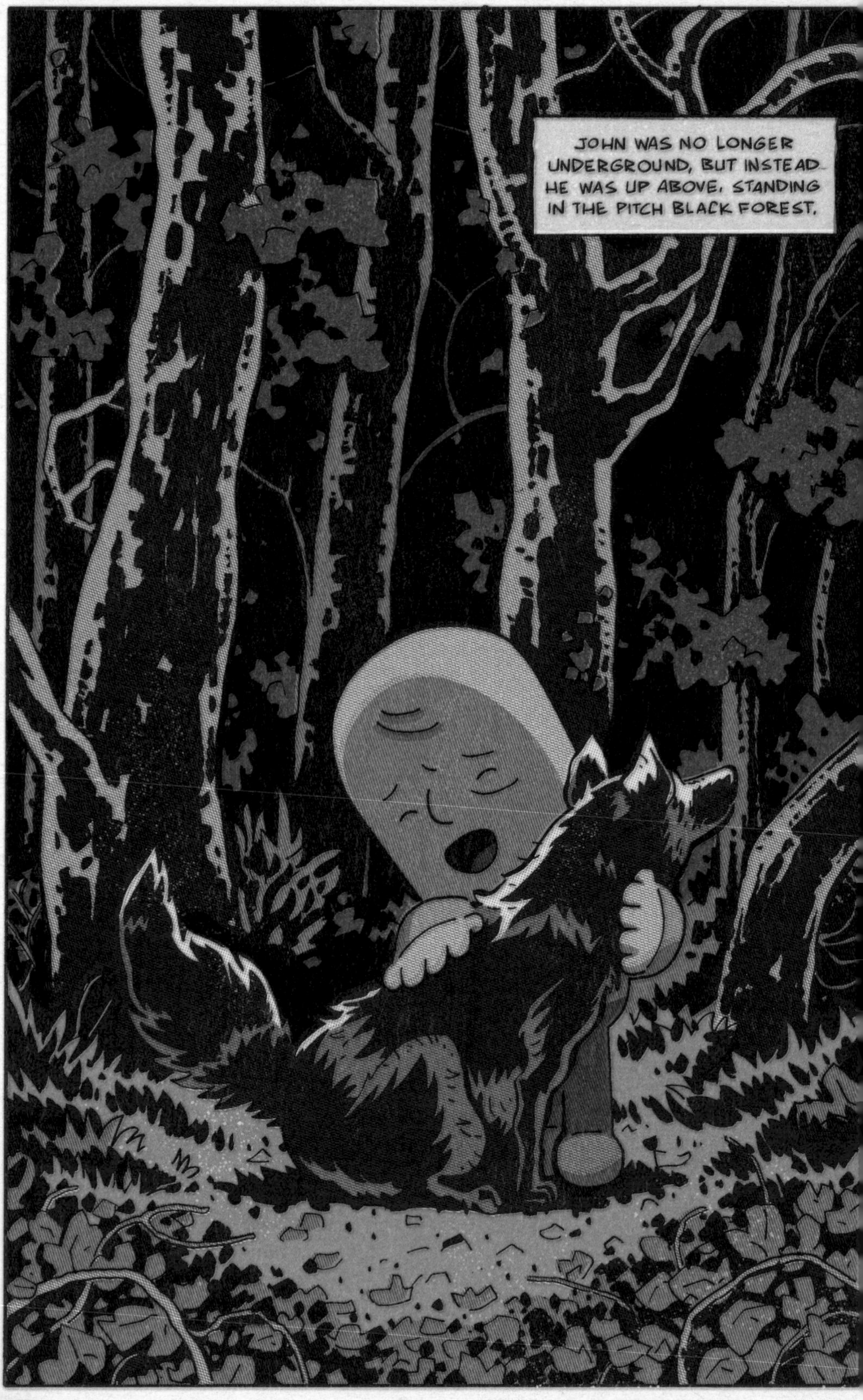
JOHN WAS NO LONGER UNDERGROUND, BUT INSTEAD HE WAS UP ABOVE, STANDING IN THE PITCH BLACK FOREST.

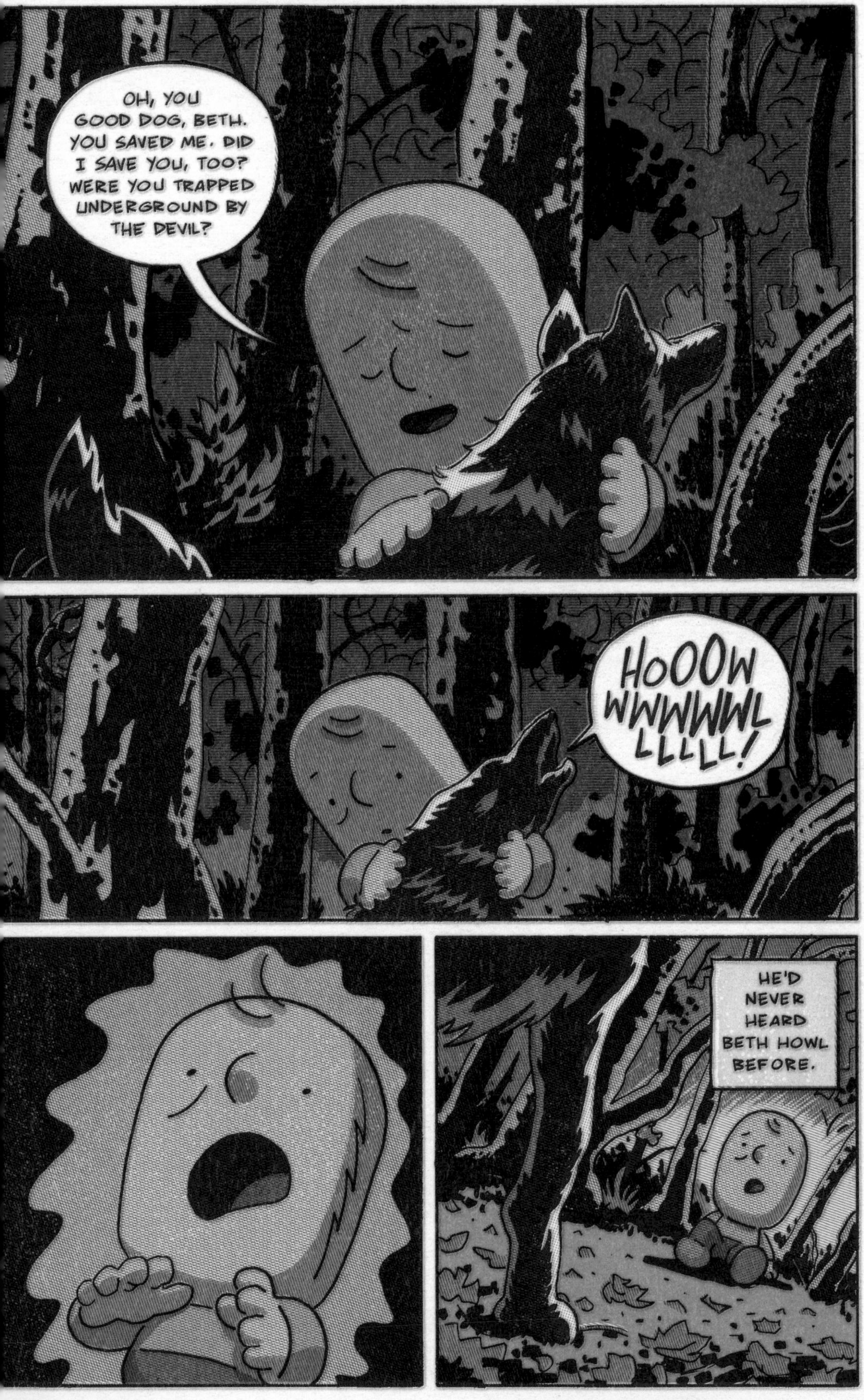
OH, YOU GOOD DOG, BETH. YOU SAVED ME. DID I SAVE YOU, TOO? WERE YOU TRAPPED UNDERGROUND BY THE DEVIL?
HoOOW WWWWWL LLLLL!
HE'D NEVER HEARD BETH HOWL BEFORE.

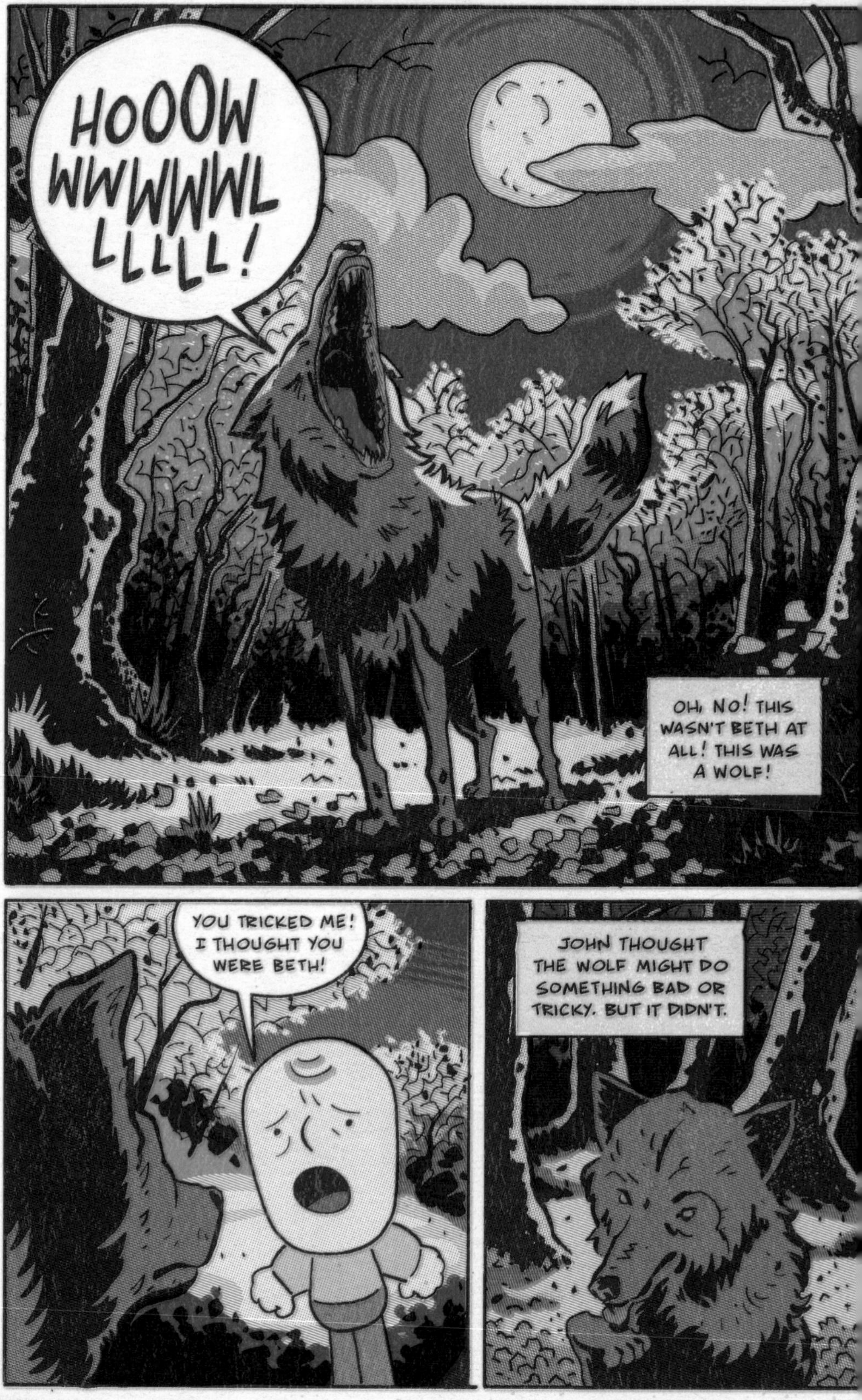
HOOOW WWWWWL LLLLL!
OH, NO! THIS WASN'T BETH AT ALL! THIS WAS A WOLF!
YOU TRICKED ME! I THOUGHT YOU WERE BETH!
JOHN THOUGHT THE WOLF MIGHT DO SOMETHING BAD OR TRICKY. BUT IT DIDN'T.

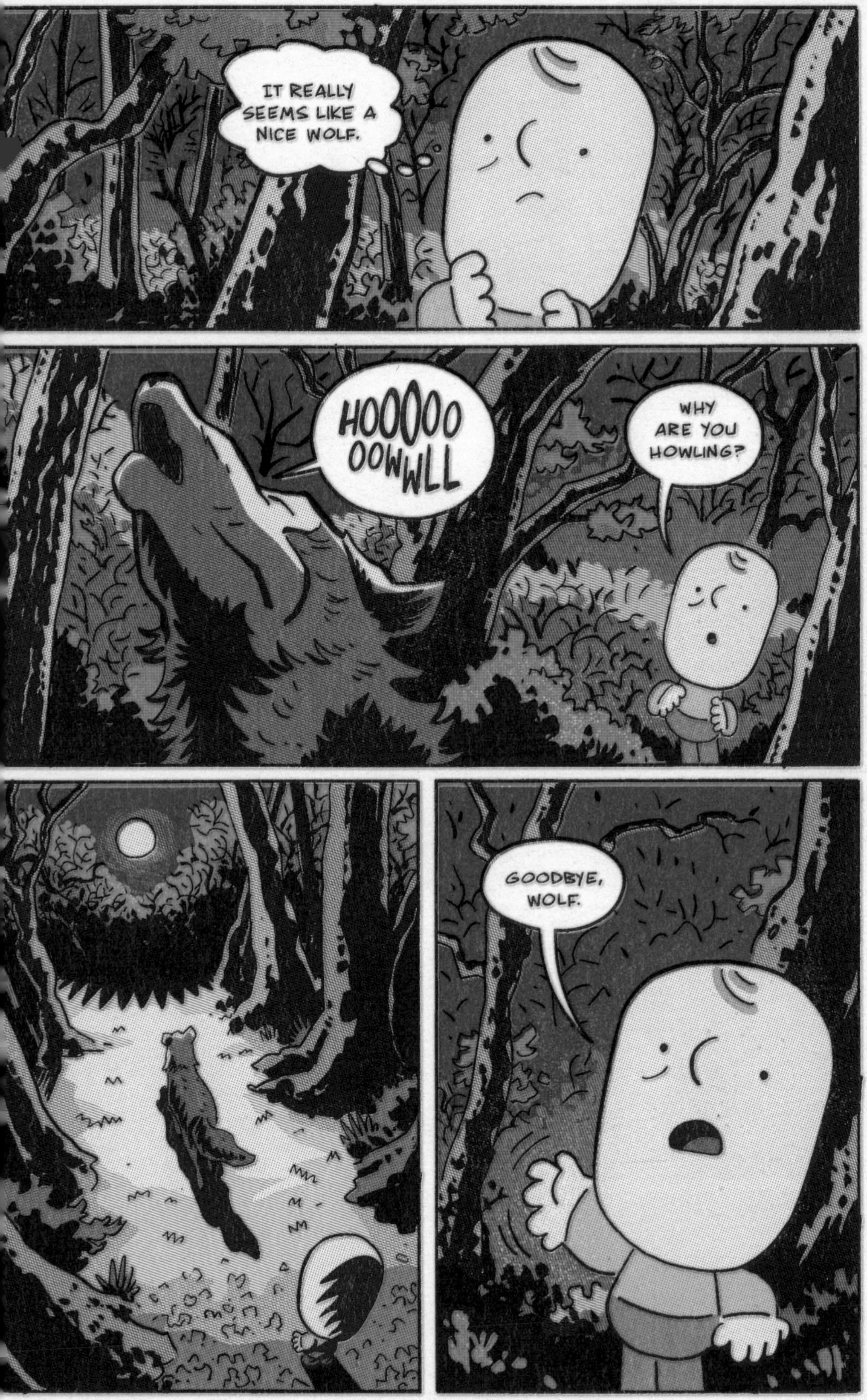
IT REALLY SEEMS LIKE A NICE WOLF.
HOOOOO OOWWLL
WHY ARE YOU HOWLING?
GOODBYE, WOLF.

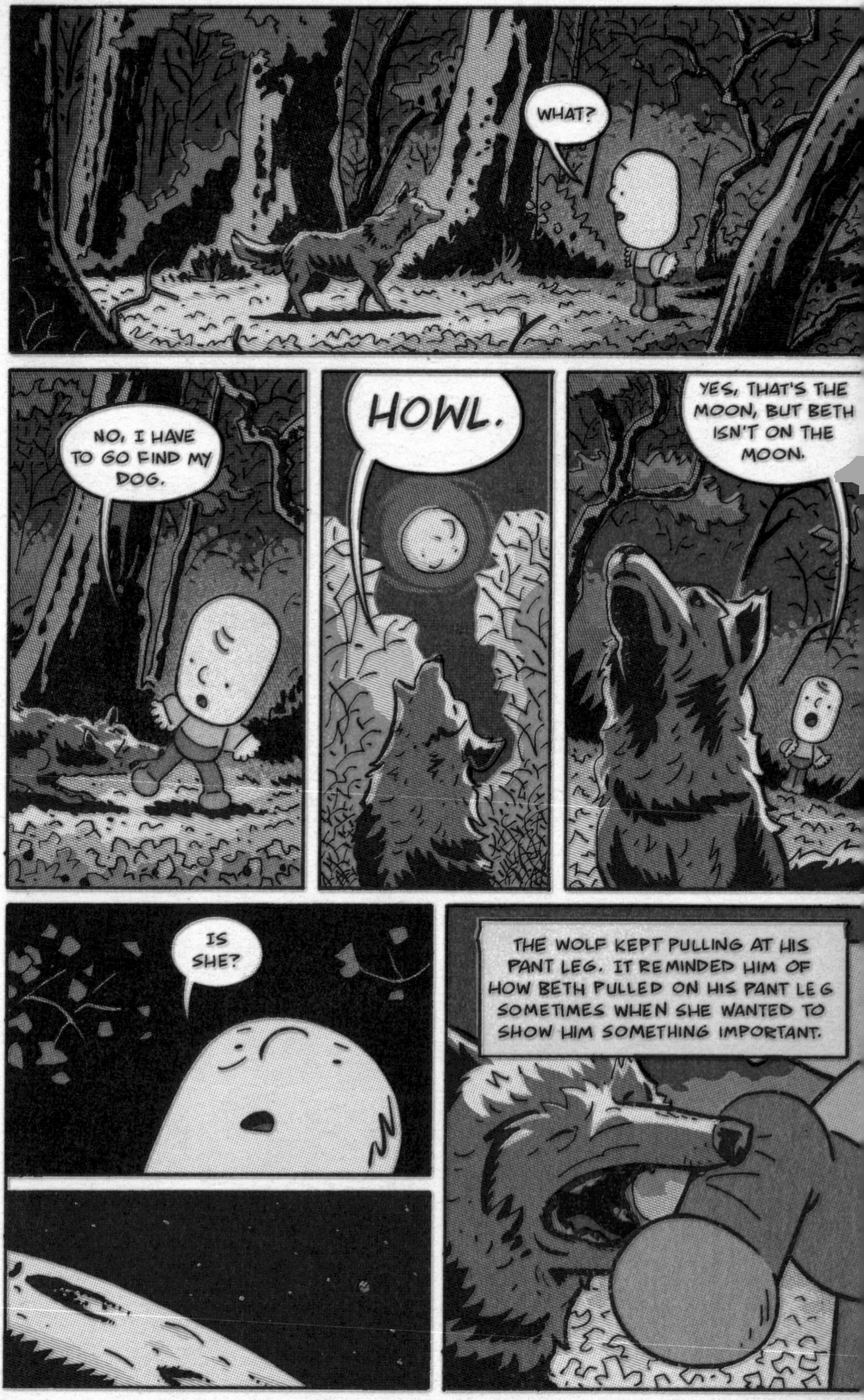
WHAT?
NO, I HAVE TO GO FIND MY DOG.
HOWL.
YES, THAT'S THE MOON, BUT BETH ISN'T ON THE MOON.
IS SHE?
THE WOLF KEPT PULLING AT HIS PANT LEG. IT REMINDED HIM OF HOW BETH PULLED ON HIS PANT LEG SOMETIMES WHEN SHE WANTED TO SHOW HIM SOMETHING IMPORTANT.

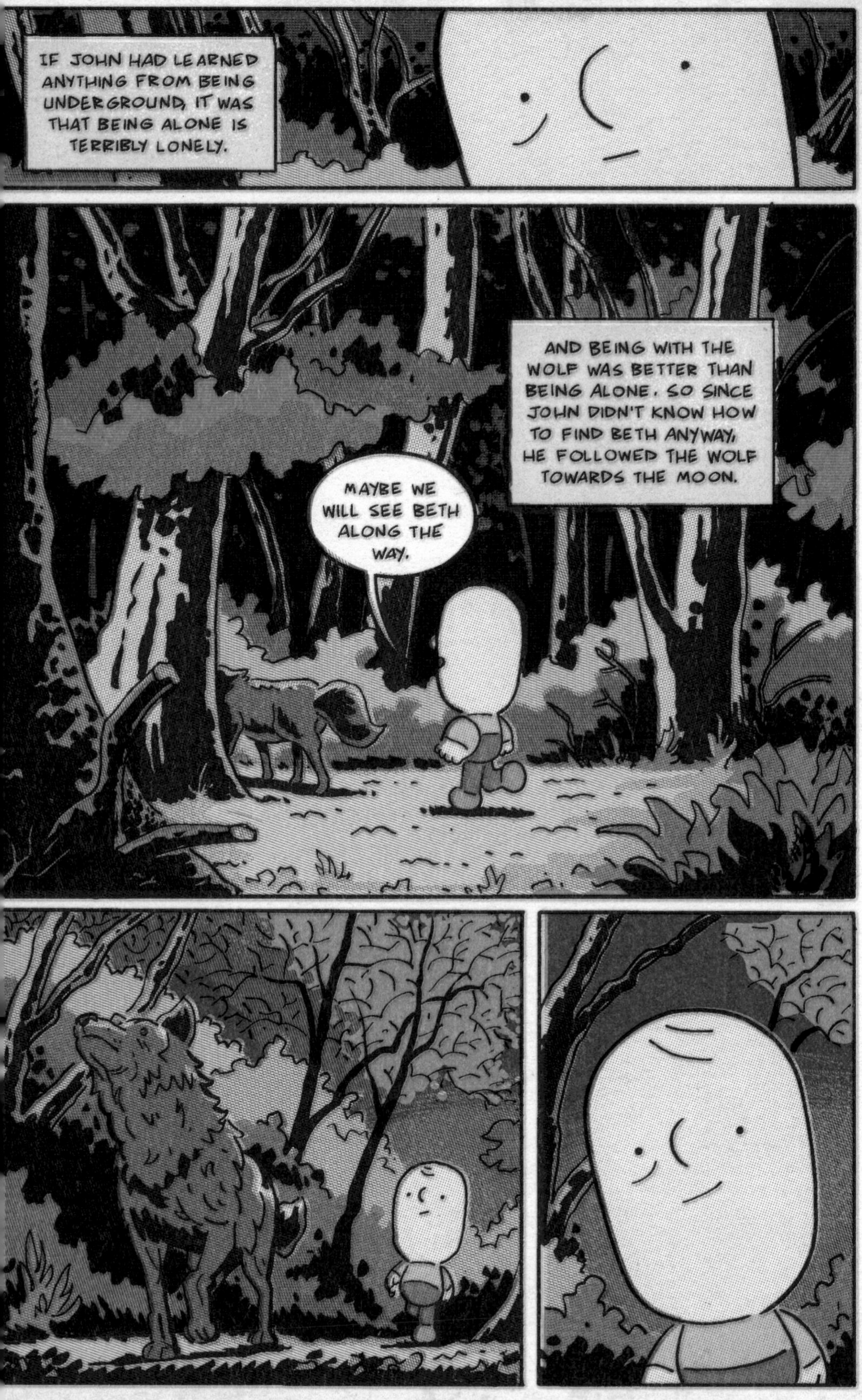
IF JOHN HAD LEARNED ANYTHING FROM BEING UNDERGROUND, IT WAS THAT BEING ALONE IS TERRIBLY LONELY.
AND BEING WITH THE WOLF WAS BETTER THAN BEING ALONE. SO SINCE JOHN DIDN'T KNOW HOW TO FIND BETH ANYWAY, HE FOLLOWED THE WOLF TOWARDS THE MOON.
MAYBE WE WILL SEE BETH ALONG THE WAY.

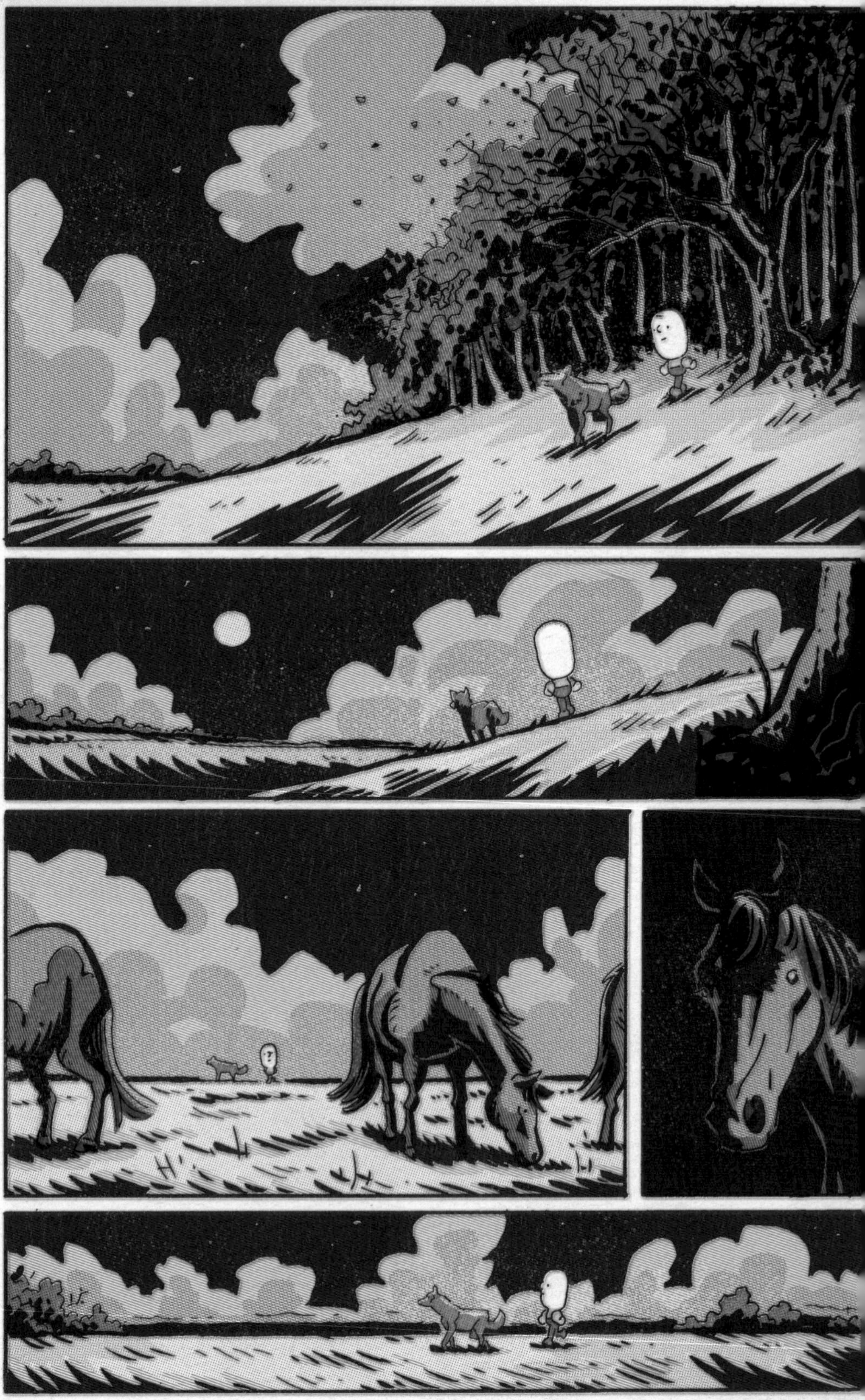

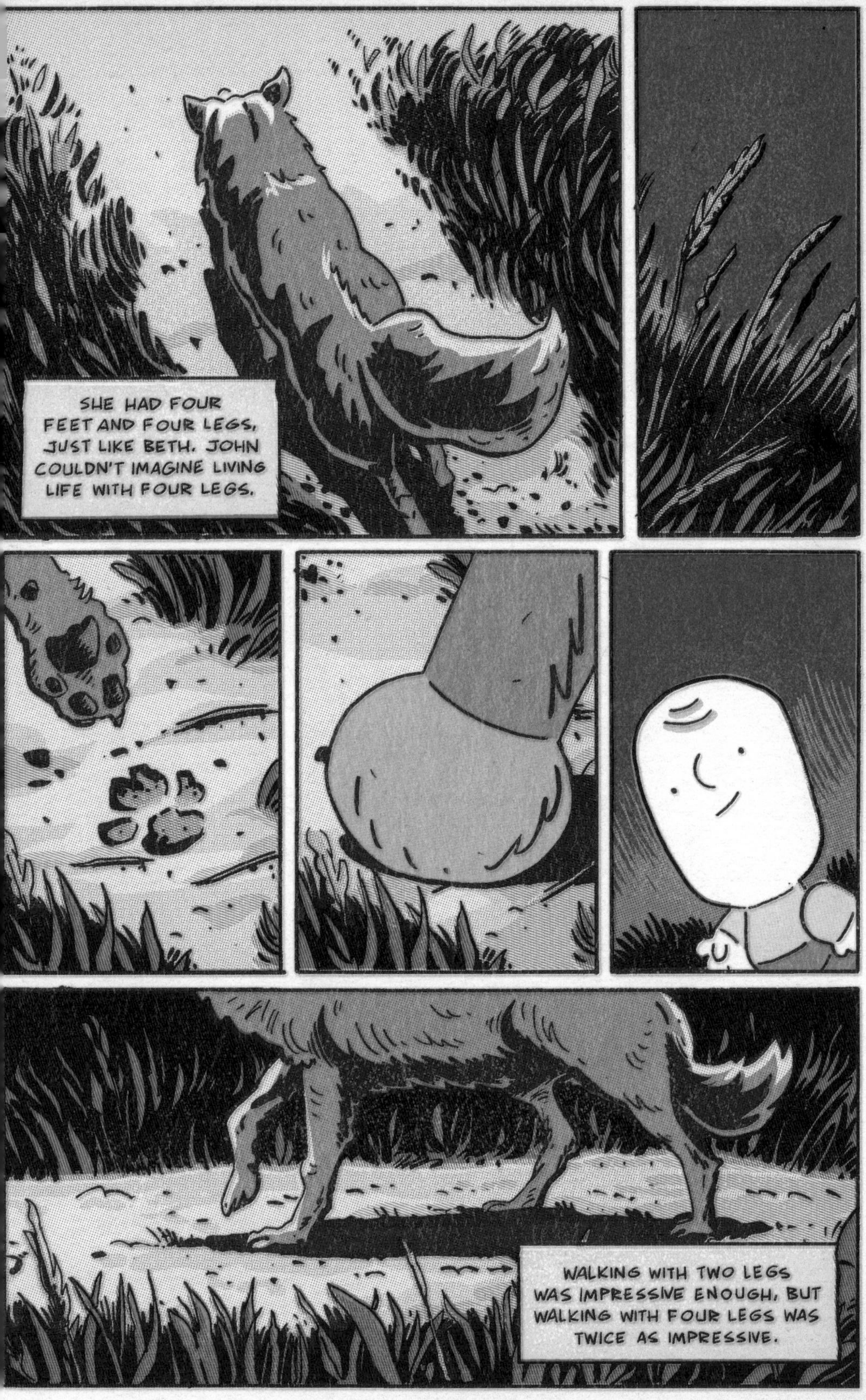
SHE HAD FOUR FEET AND FOUR LEGS, JUST LIKE BETH. JOHN COULDN'T IMAGINE LIVING LIFE WITH FOUR LEGS.
WALKING WITH TWO LEGS WAS IMPRESSIVE ENOUGH, BUT WALKING WITH FOUR LEGS WAS TWICE AS IMPRESSIVE.

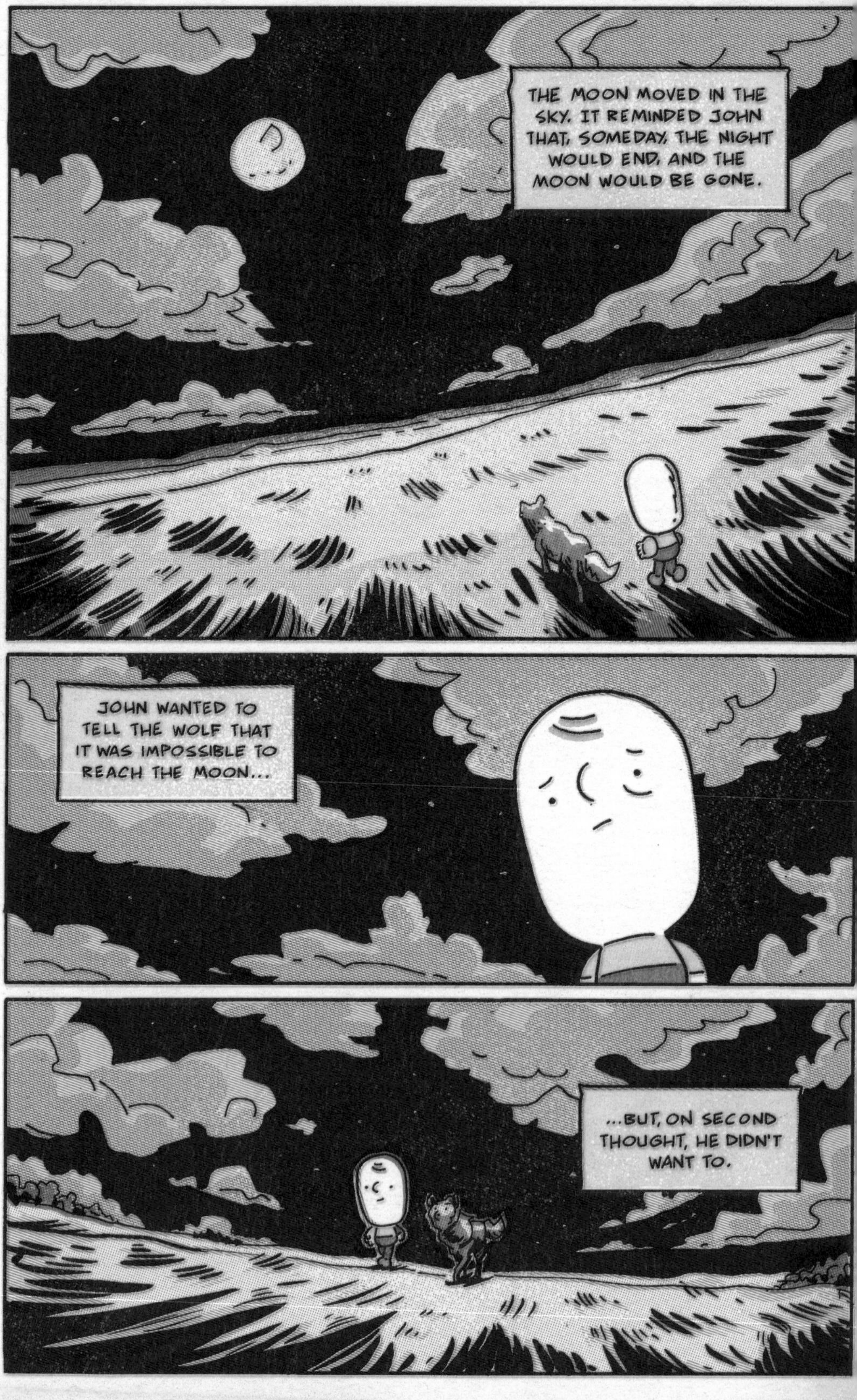
THE MOON MOVED IN THE SKY. IT REMINDED JOHN THAT, SOMEDAY, THE NIGHT WOULD END, AND THE MOON WOULD BE GONE.
JOHN WANTED TO TELL THE WOLF THAT IT WAS IMPOSSIBLE TO REACH THE MOON...
...BUT, ON SECOND THOUGHT, HE DIDN'T WANT TO.

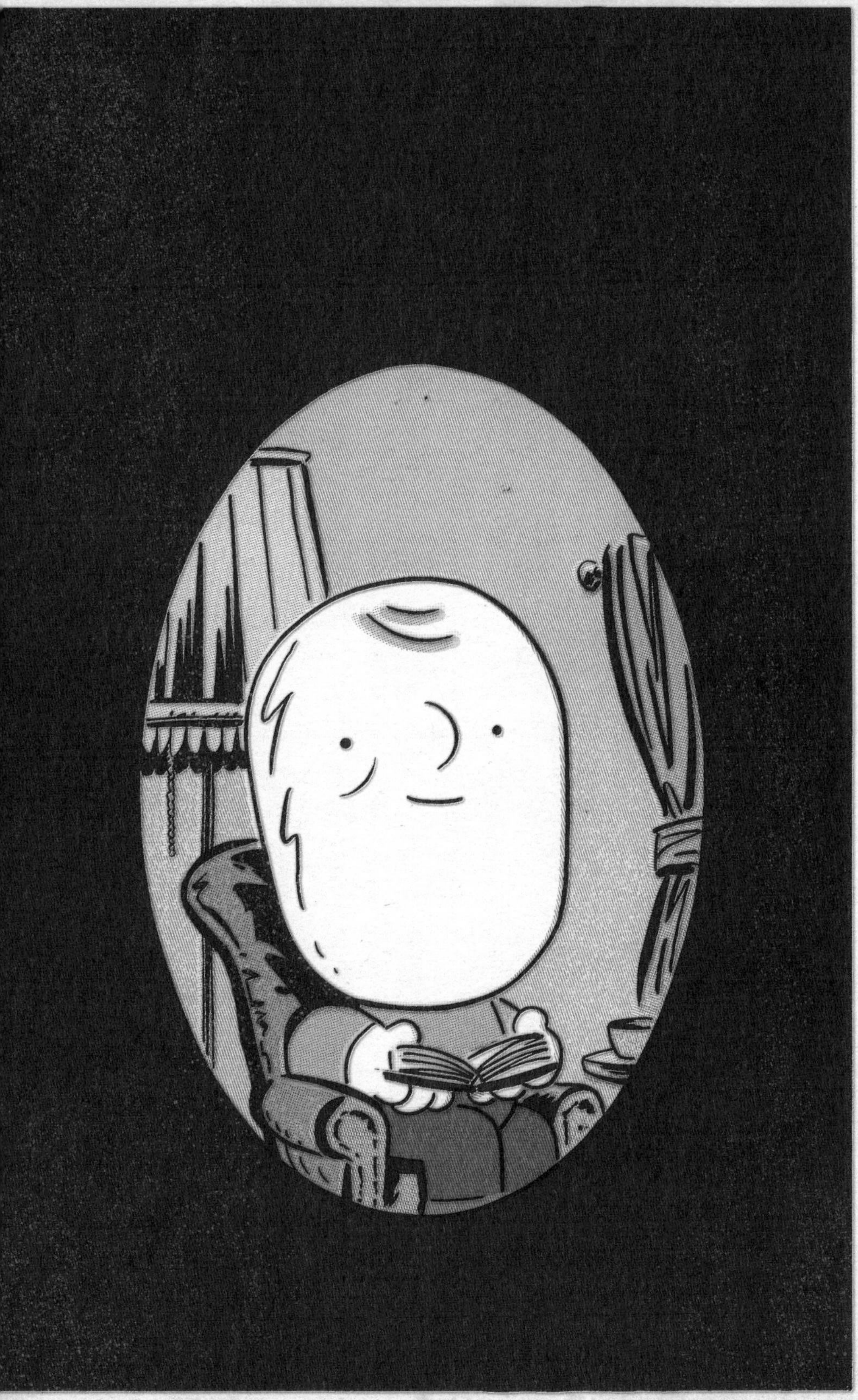

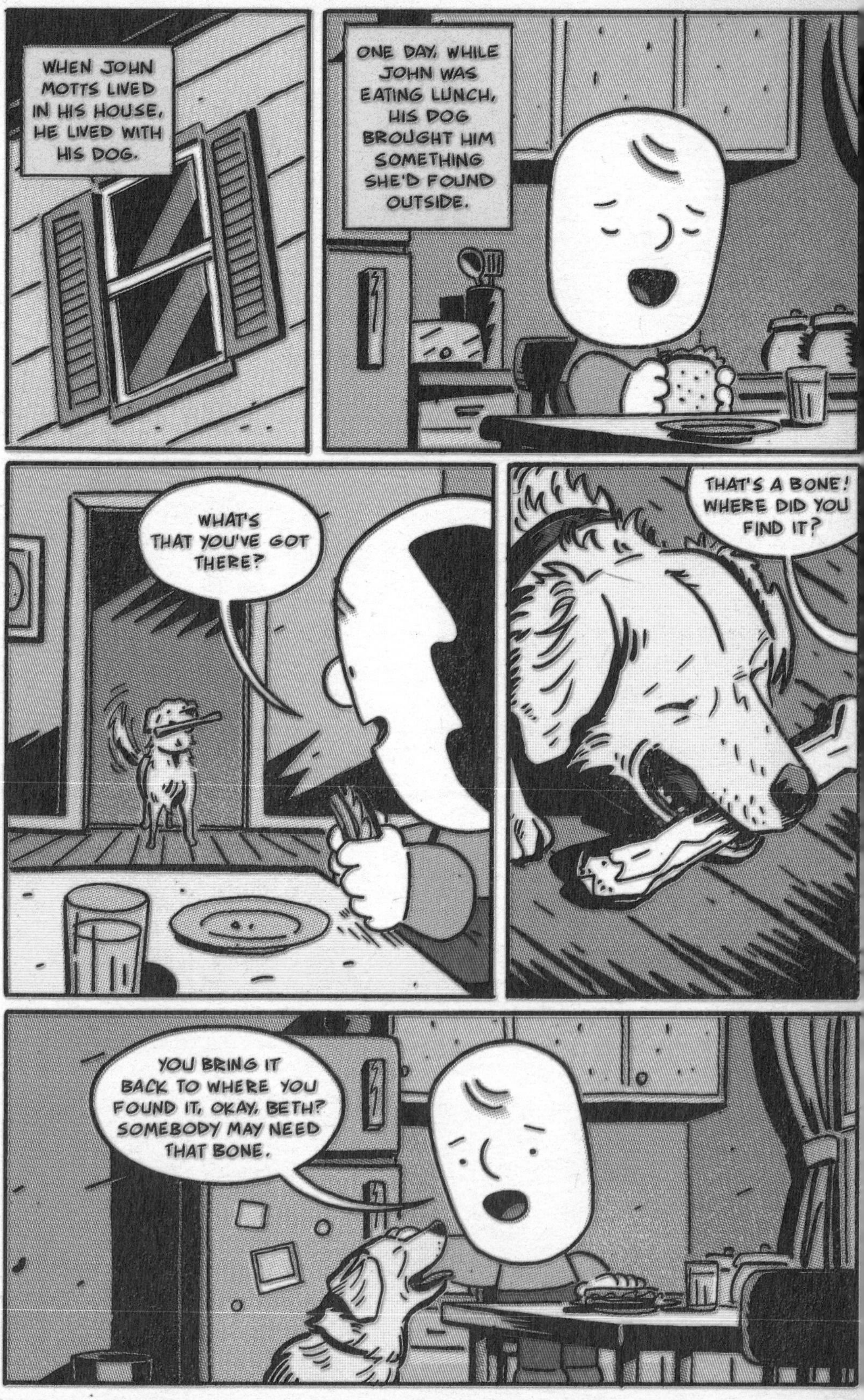
WHEN JOHN MOTTS LIVED IN HIS HOUSE, HE LIVED WITH HIS DOG.
ONE DAY, WHILE JOHN WAS EATING LUNCH, HIS DOG BROUGHT HIM SOMETHING SHE'D FOUND OUTSIDE.
WHAT'S THAT YOU'VE GOT THERE?
THAT'S A BONE! WHERE DID YOU FIND IT?
YOU BRING IT BACK TO WHERE YOU FOUND IT, OKAY, BETH? SOMEBODY MAY NEED THAT BONE.

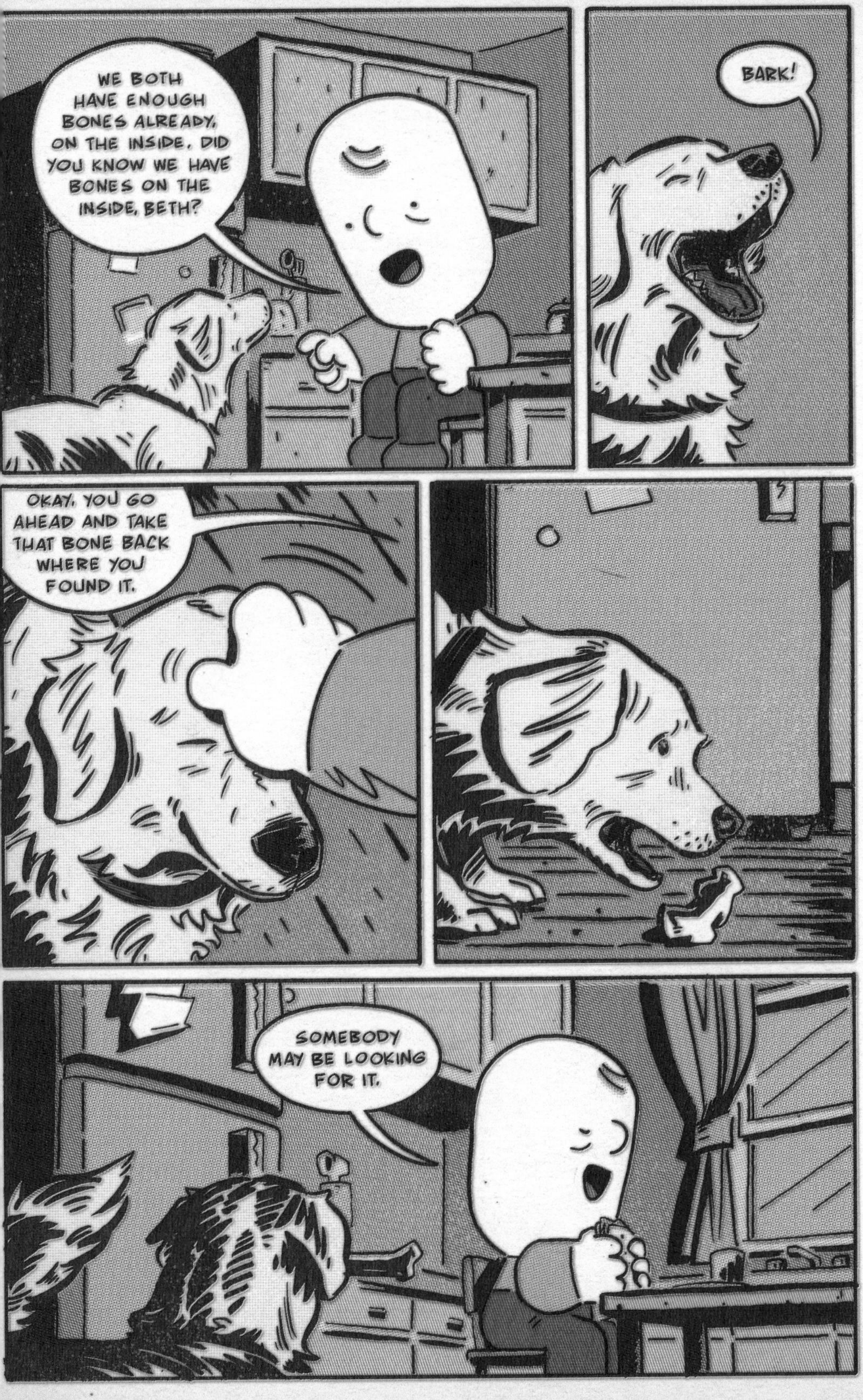
WE BOTH HAVE ENOUGH BONES ALREADY, ON THE INSIDE. DID YOU KNOW WE HAVE BONES ON THE INSIDE, BETH?
BARK!
OKAY. YOU GO AHEAD AND TAKE THAT BONE BACK WHERE YOU FOUND IT.
SOMEBODY MAY BE LOOKING FOR IT.

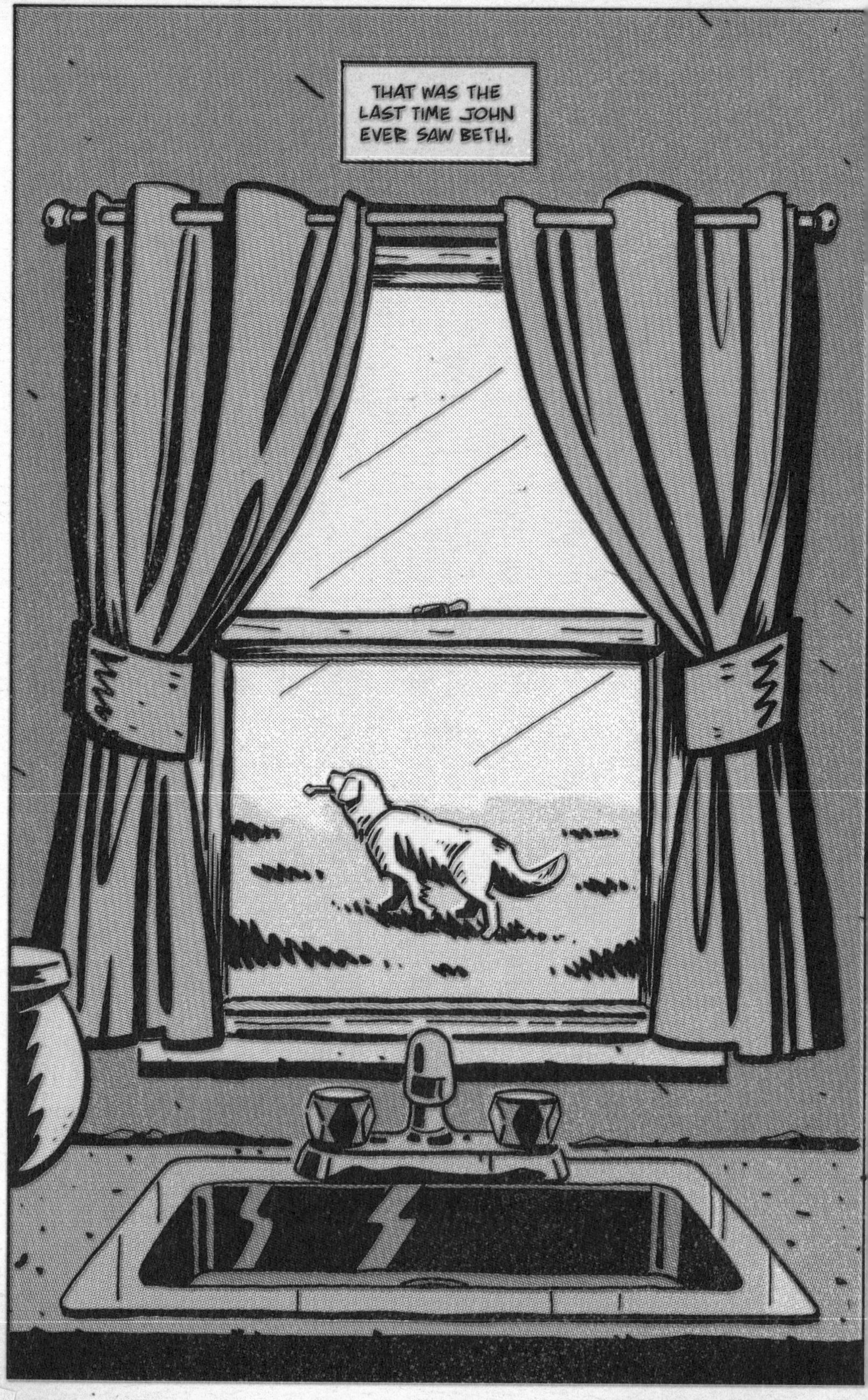
THAT WAS THE LAST TIME JOHN EVER SAW BETH.

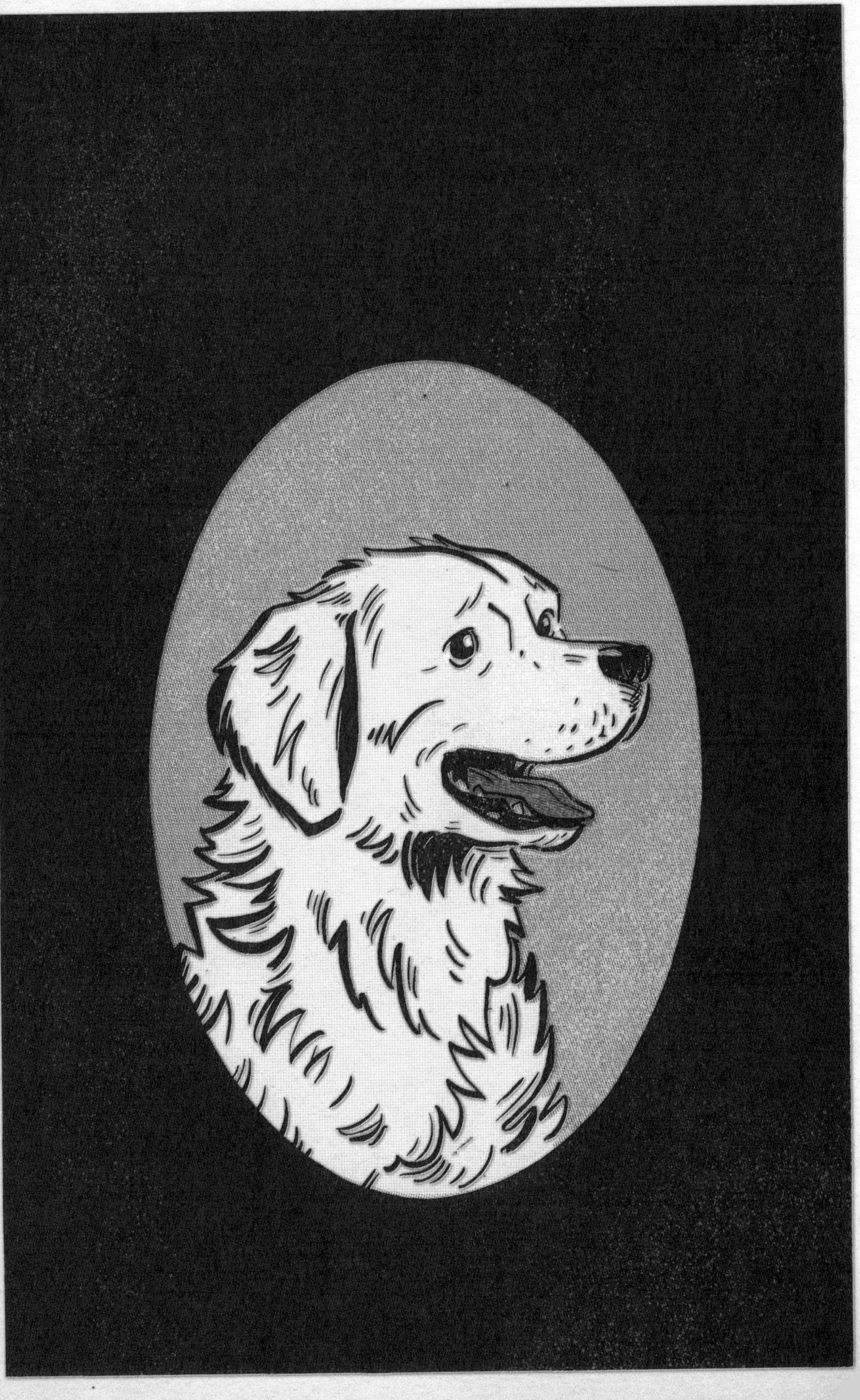

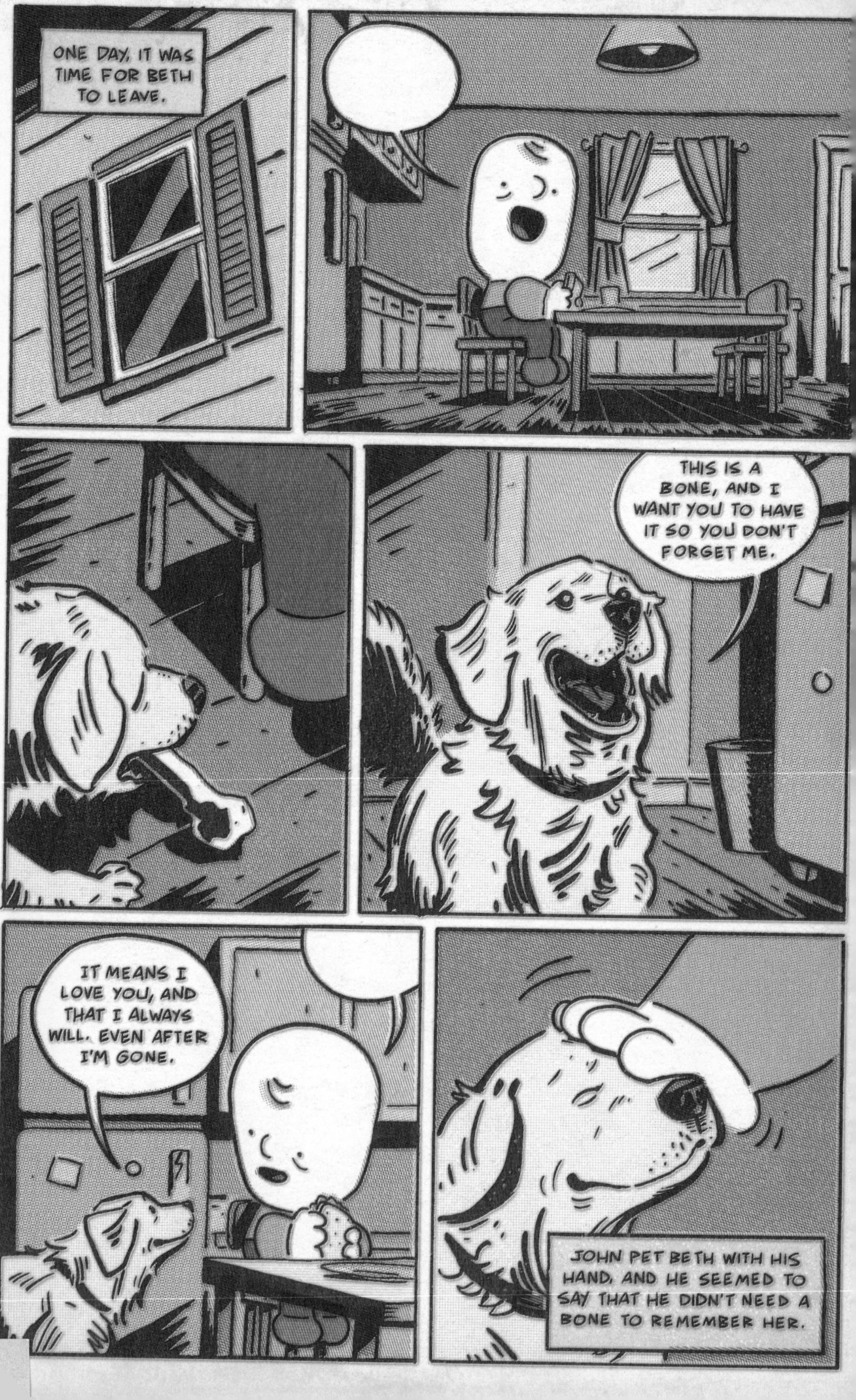
ONE DAY, IT WAS TIME FOR BETH TO LEAVE.
THIS IS A BONE, AND I WANT YOU TO HAVE IT SO YOU DON'T FORGET ME.
IT MEANS I LOVE YOU, AND THAT I ALWAYS WILL. EVEN AFTER I'M GONE.
JOHN PET BETH WITH HIS HAND, AND HE SEEMED TO SAY THAT HE DIDN'T NEED A BONE TO REMEMBER HER.

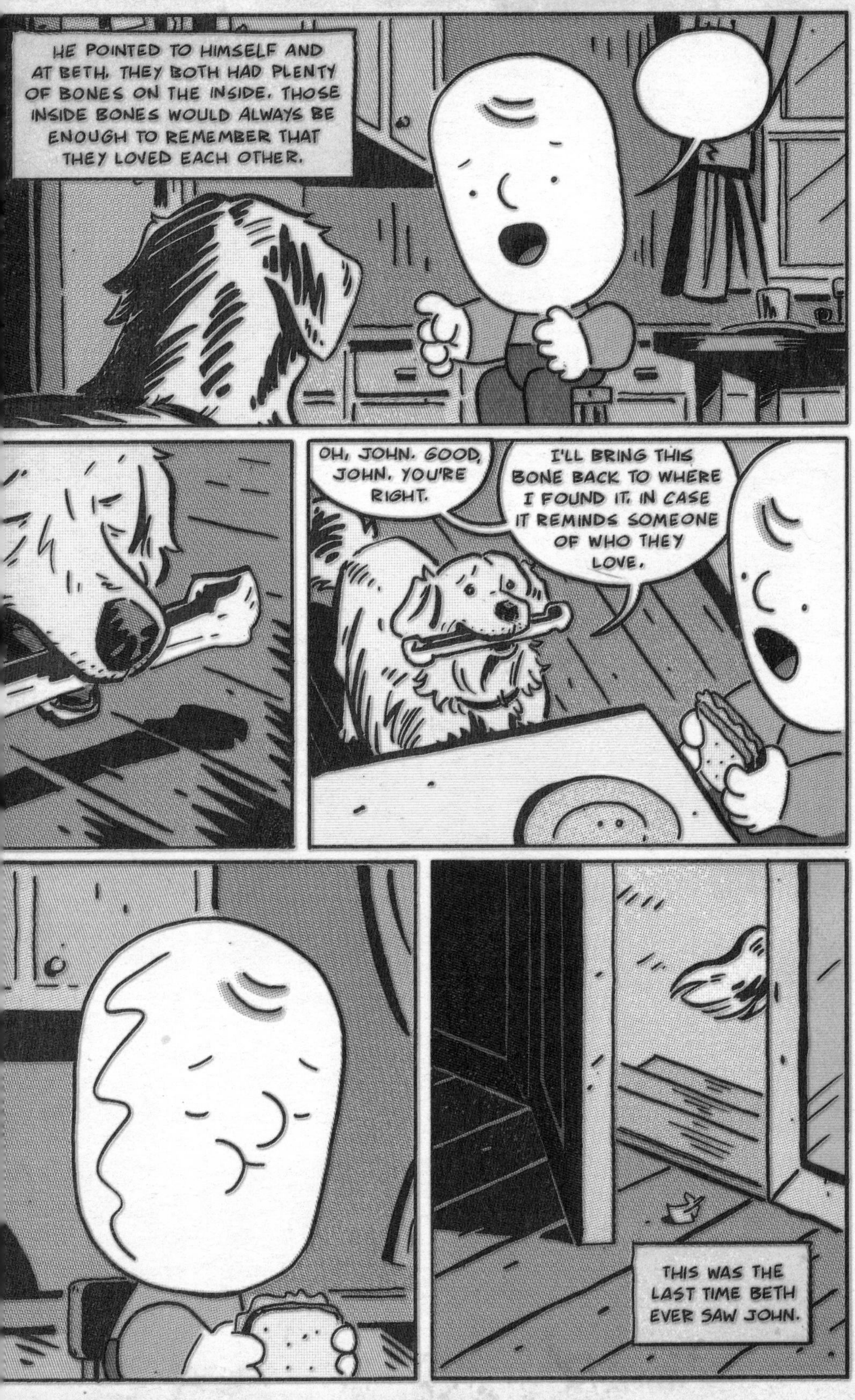
HE POINTED TO HIMSELF AND AT BETH. THEY BOTH HAD PLENTY OF BONES ON THE INSIDE. THOSE INSIDE BONES WOULD ALWAYS BE ENOUGH TO REMEMBER THAT THEY LOVED EACH OTHER.
OH, JOHN. GOOD, JOHN. YOU'RE RIGHT.
I'LL BRING THIS BONE BACK TO WHERE I FOUND IT. IN CASE IT REMINDS SOMEONE OF WHO THEY LOVE.
THIS WAS THE LAST TIME BETH EVER SAW JOHN.

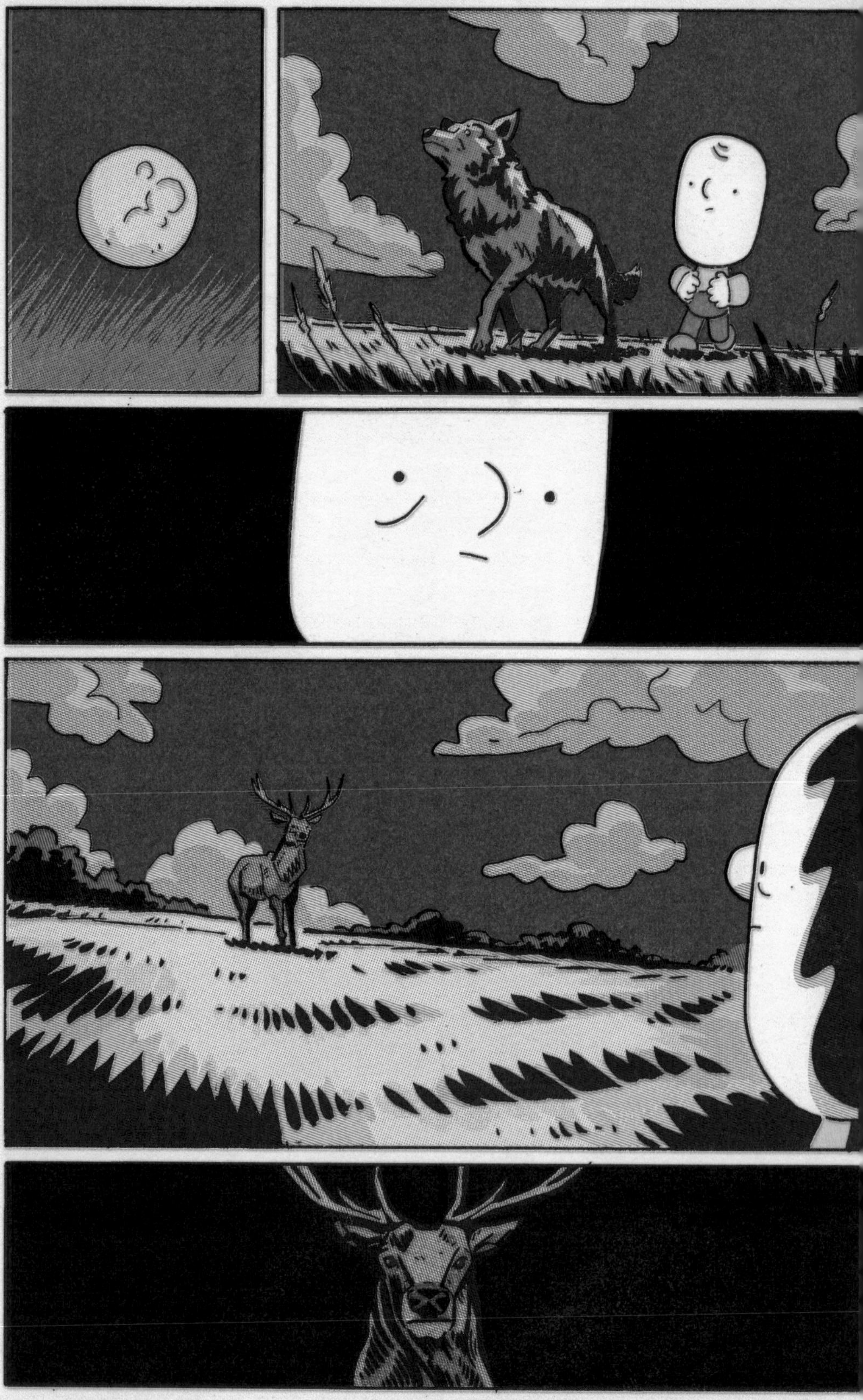

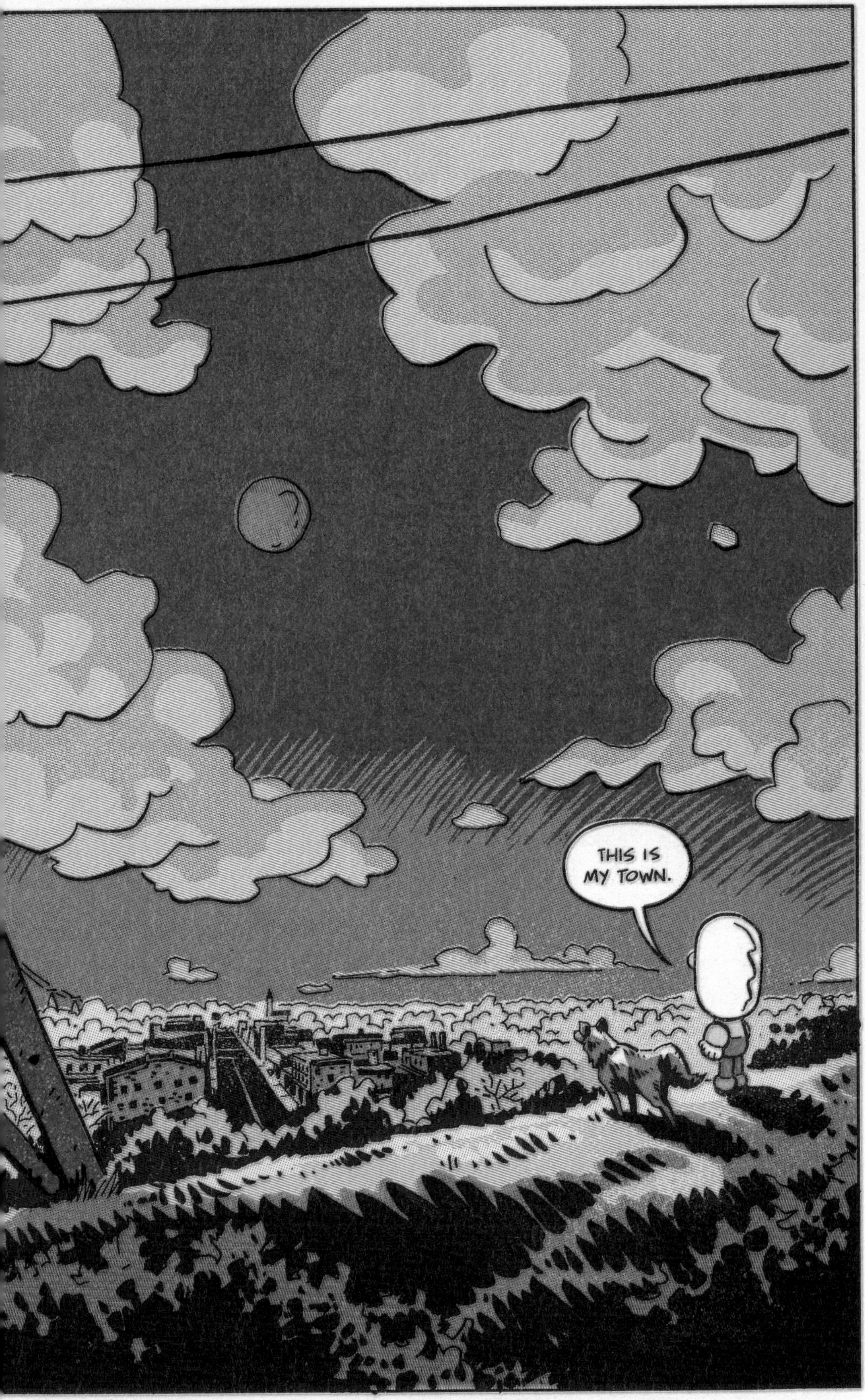
THIS IS MY TOWN.

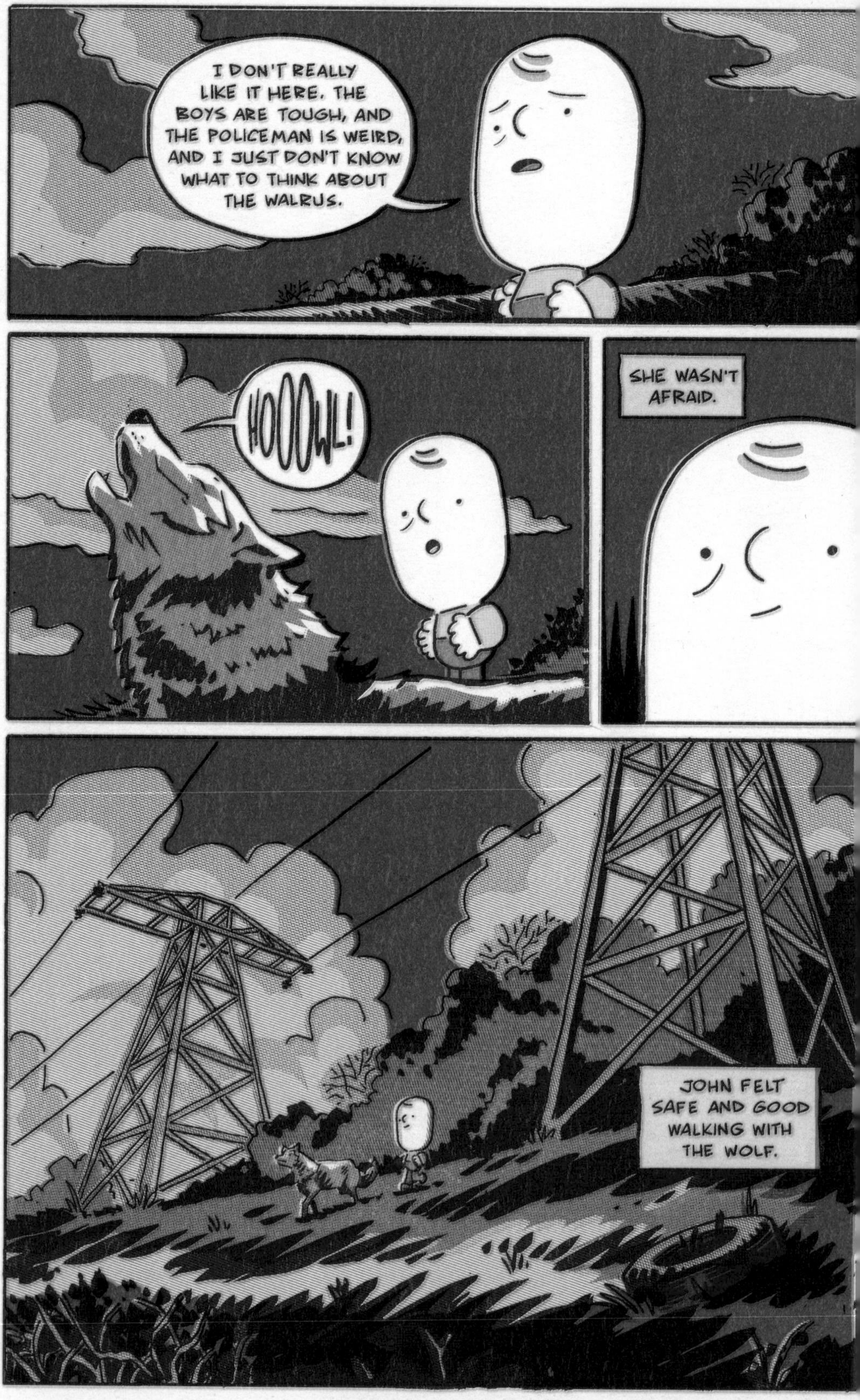
I DON'T REALLY LIKE IT HERE. THE BOYS ARE TOUGH, AND THE POLICEMAN IS WEIRD, AND I JUST DON'T KNOW WHAT TO THINK ABOUT THE WALRUS.
HOOOWL!
SHE WASN'T AFRAID.
JOHN FELT SAFE AND GOOD WALKING WITH THE WOLF.

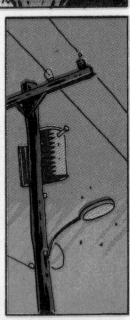

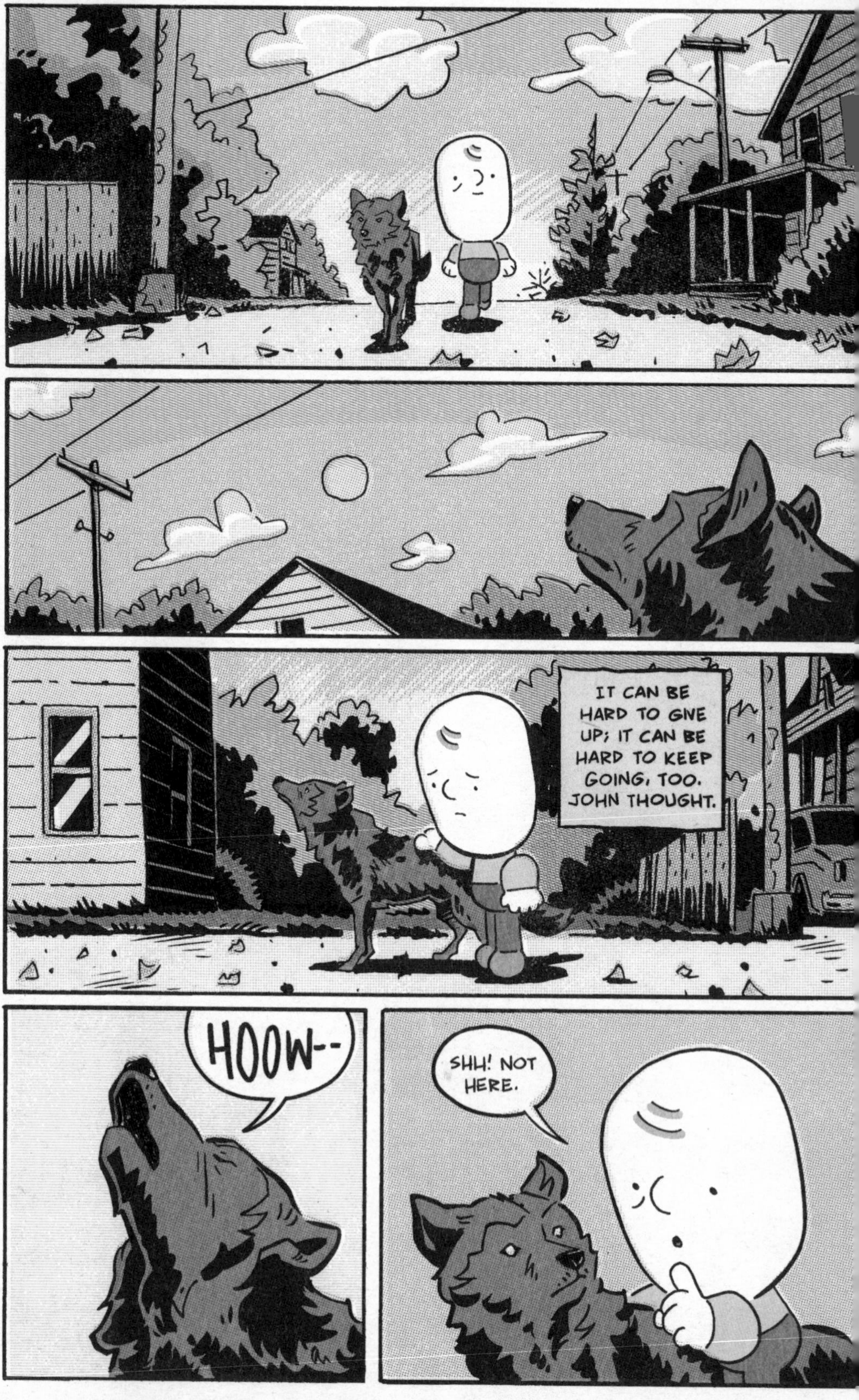
IT CAN BE HARD TO GIVE UP; IT CAN BE HARD TO KEEP GOING, TOO. JOHN THOUGHT.
HOOW--
SHH! NOT HERE.

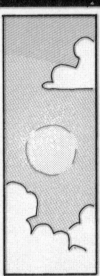

WE DON'T HAVE TO REACH THE MOON TODAY, Y'KNOW. WE CAN TRY AGAIN TONIGHT OR TOMORROW NIGHT.

IT'LL BE A DIFFERENT SHAPE, BUT IT'LL STILL BE THE MOON.

THE MOON CHANGES EVERY NIGHT. DID YOU KNOW THAT?

C'MON. LET'S HEAD HOME, GIRL. DO YOU LIKE DOG FOOD?

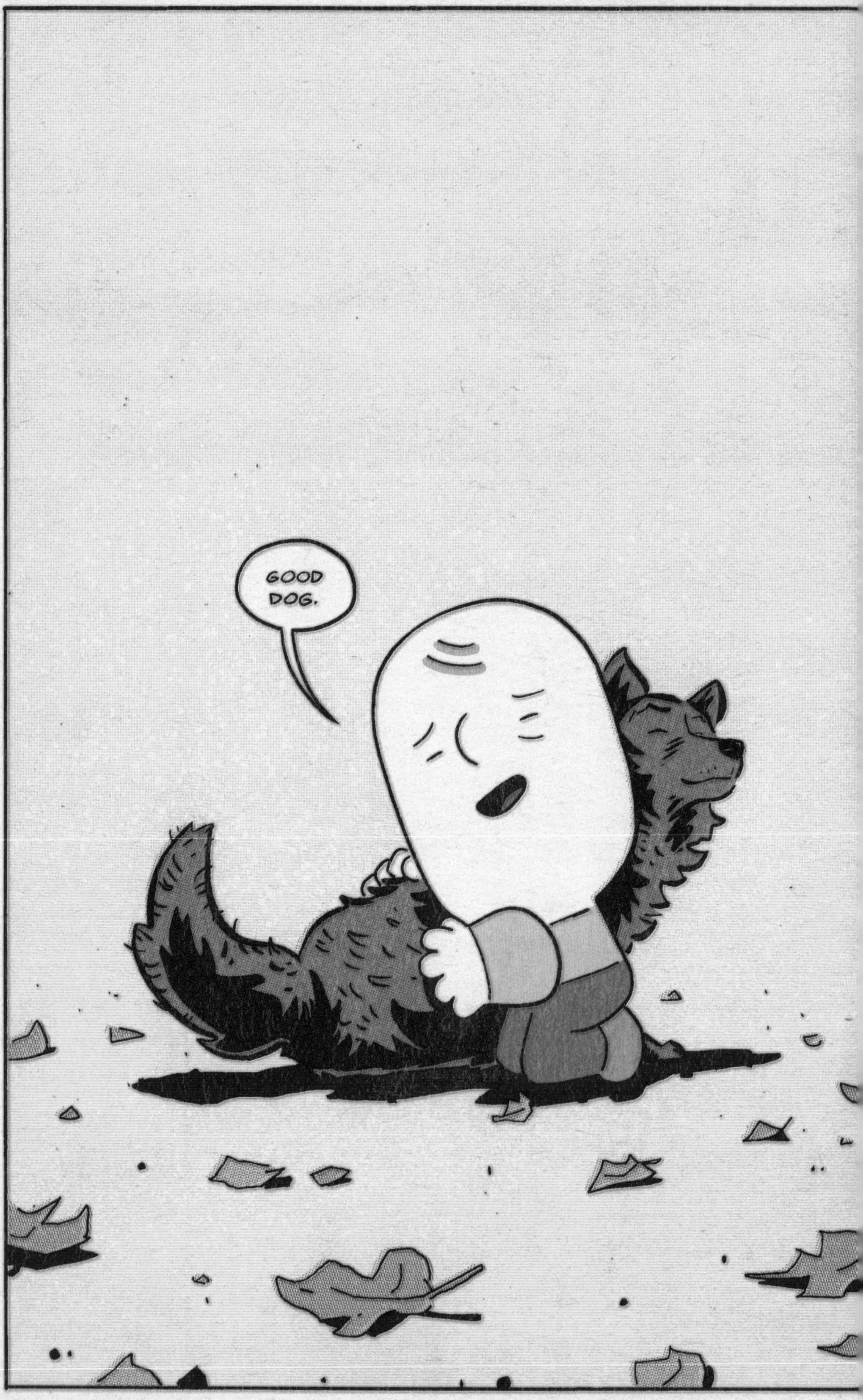
GOOD DOG.

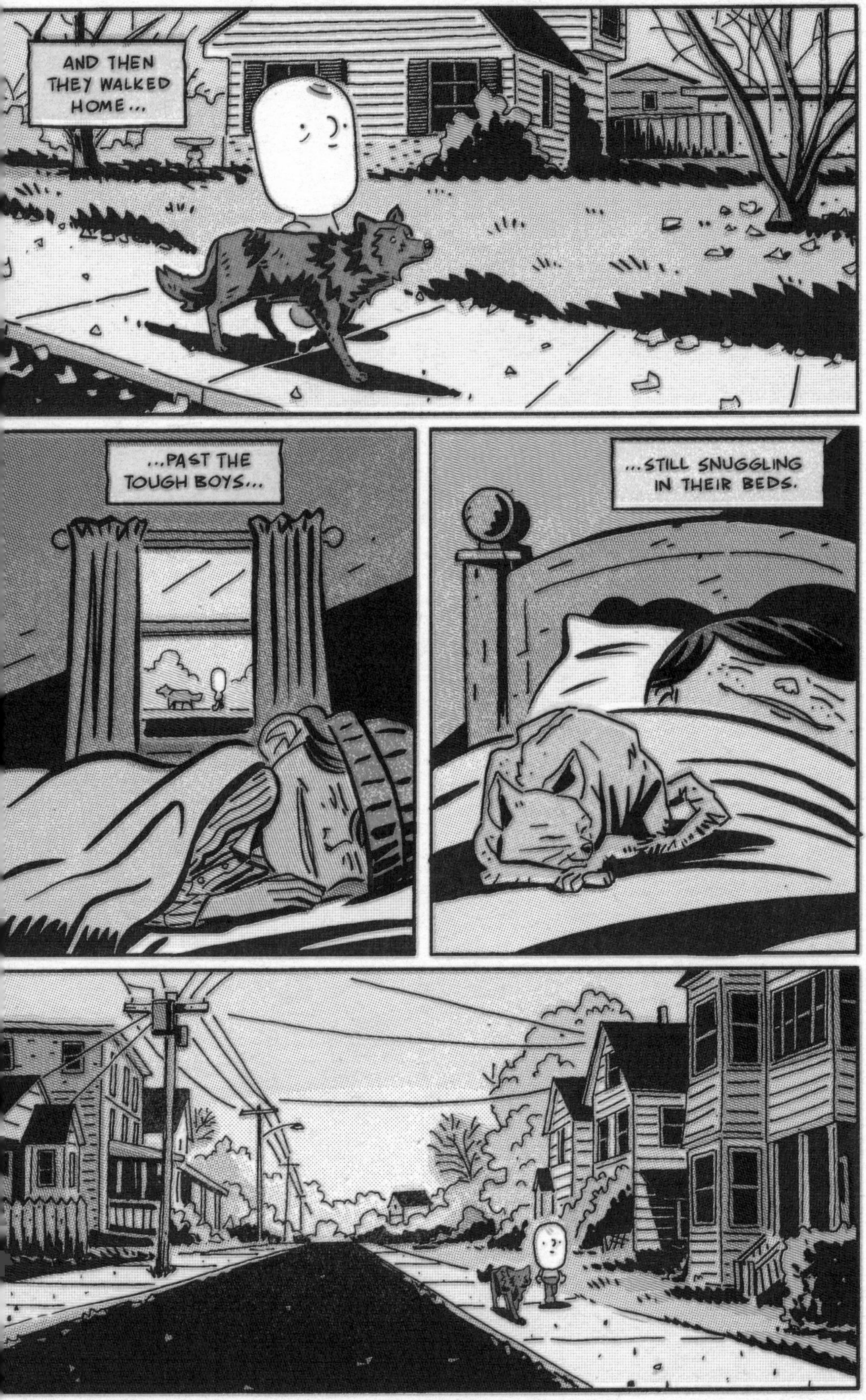
AND THEN THEY WALKED HOME...
...PAST THE TOUGH BOYS...
...STILL SNUGGLING IN THEIR BEDS.

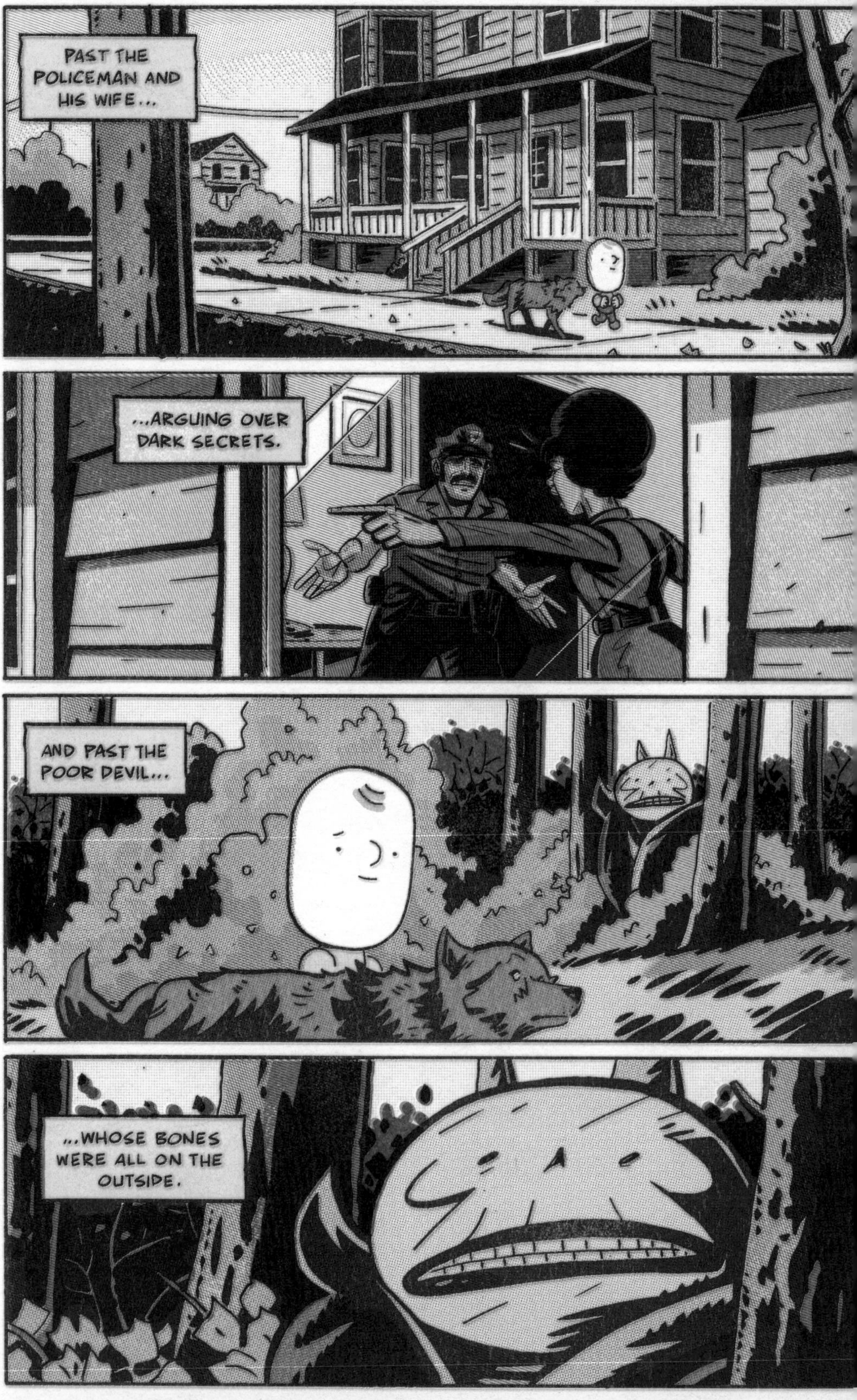
PAST THE POLICEMAN AND HIS WIFE...
...ARGUING OVER DARK SECRETS.
AND PAST THE POOR DEVIL...
...WHOSE BONES WERE ALL ON THE OUTSIDE.

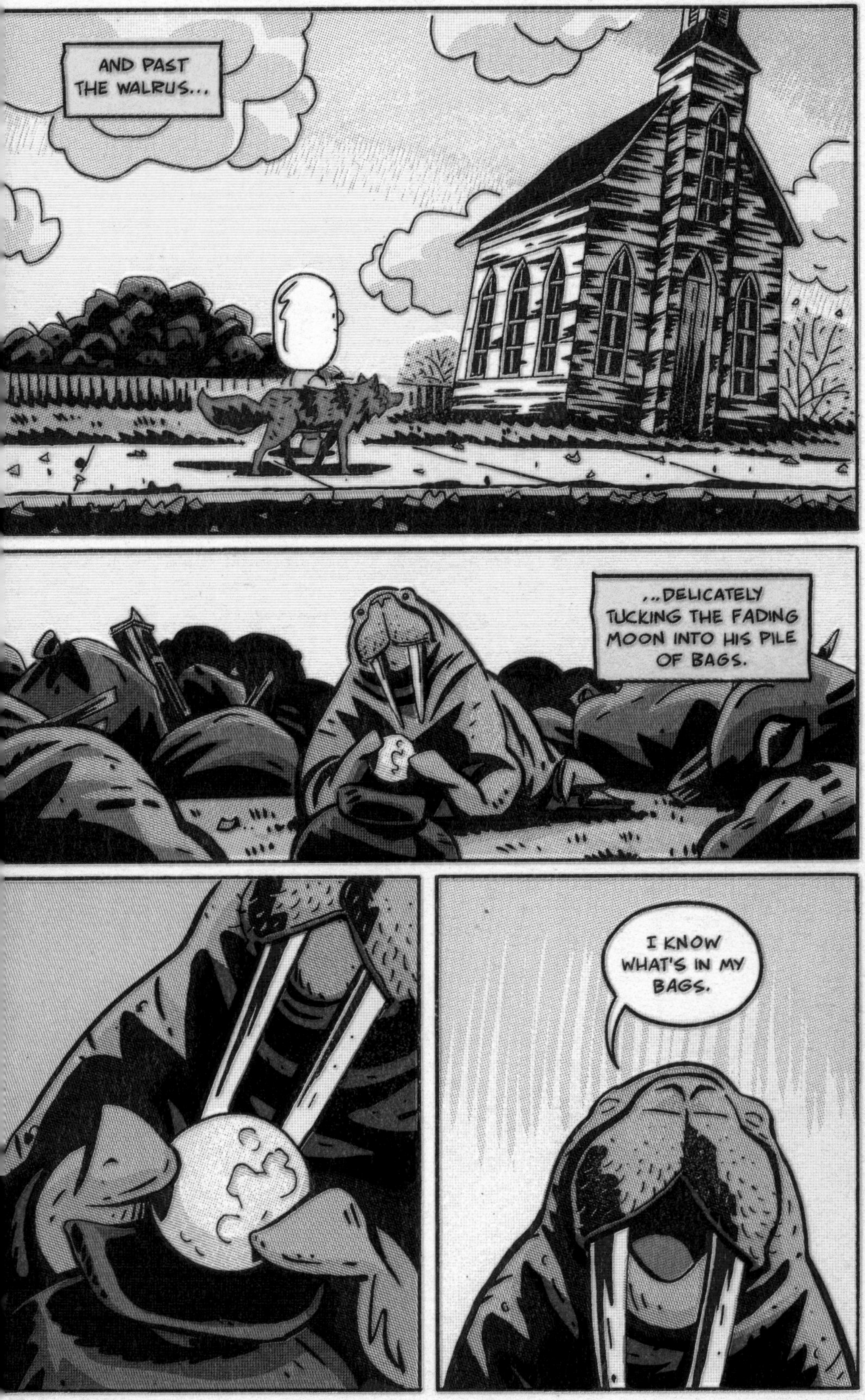
AND PAST THE WALRUS...
...DELICATELY TUCKING THE FADING MOON INTO HIS PILE OF BAGS.
I KNOW WHAT'S IN MY BAGS.

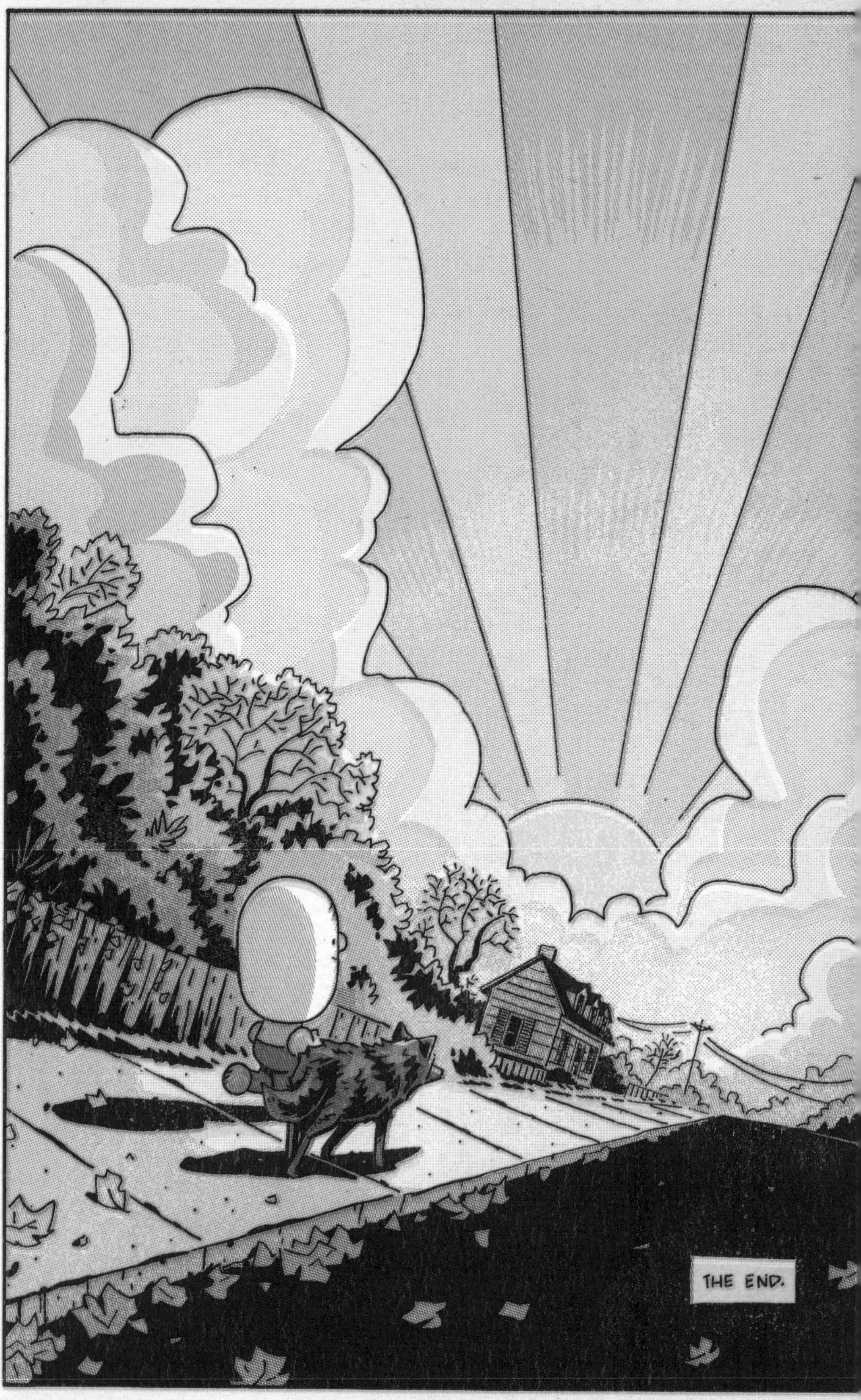
THE END.

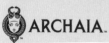